"There's nobody I've met in my life who had as much engineering expertise as Alvin. He was the smartest and most gifted engineer I've ever known, and, I daresay, perhaps the engineering profession has ever seen."

—Bob Benz, owner, Benz Engineering

"As far as intelligence, Alvin's was the sharpest mind I've ever met. He was a genius who knew a little bit about everything. He was also a real character."

—Lanny Trefz, owner, LRT Racing Engines

"I was at Al's house sometimes when his business partners would show up. I could see how they were all very respectful of him and treated him like a guru. He was an absolutely brilliant engineer."

—Chris Boehr, software engineer

"I believe Al was one of the great thinkers and writers in the field of human interaction in society. I can't say enough about the intellectual stimulation and challenge he gave me."

—John Goode, orthodontist

"Al was known for his rigorous scientific knowledge and his brilliance in physics, but he also had a visionary quality about him that was quite poetic. He was able to talk about the invisible world in a physical and scientific language that made it more beautiful."

—Sara Taft, author of *Mary Magdalene, Shaman*

"I have a master's degree in nuclear engineering but it took Al to show me the beauty of thorium reactors. He emphasized the importance of the scientific method as the way to find truth and learn more about the world. I wouldn't be where I am today if he hadn't crossed my path."

—John Imig, owner, Imig Industries

"Al was a prolific writer. He was gifted in the way he expressed himself. His approach was informed by his views on the scientific method and he did not cater to any ideological biases. He wrote eloquently and asserted his views strongly but always respectfully."

—Bruce Canter (JD), independent legal consultant

"Two men have had a profound influence on how I view the world. Andrew Galambos introduced me to startlingly original ideas of how to solve the problems of humanity without a political structure. And Alvin Lowi found a deeper foundation for those ideas. The way he expanded on, and incorporated them, into his life, is a most compelling model for me."

—Jeff Solomon, computer hardware designer

"Alvin presented himself as a folksy guy who loved telling front porch stories. But the truth is, he was a deep scientific thinker with a profound comprehension of history, scientific epistemology, math, thermodynamics, and engineering. He was one of the smartest guys you'd ever meet."

—Chas Holloway, creator of Free World Theory

"The breadth of Al's knowledge was truly impressive. He was a legitimate genius, but if he knew it, he never let on. In addition to his formidable intellect, he was generous and hospitable to a fault. His door was always open to family and friends."

—Paul Mullen, computer engineer

ALVIN LOWI JR.
American Polymath

OTHER NONFICTION BOOKS
BY MIKE HAMEL

*The Entrepreneur's Creed: The Principles & Passions of
20 Successful Entrepreneurs*

Giving Back: Using Your Influence to Create Social Change

*Stumbling Toward Heaven: Mike Hamel on Cancer, Crashes
and Questions*

We Will Be Landing Shortly: Now What?

Social Enterprise 2.0: The OWP Difference

Spencer MacCallum: A Man Beyond His Time

ALVIN LOWI JR.
American Polymath

Mike Hamel

Mike Hamel

CONTENTS

FOREWORD

Alvin Lowi Jr. was a charismatic conversationalist and a prolific and gifted writer, so I am humbled by the request to write this foreword. Al was an inspiring mentor to me, as well as to his family, friends, colleagues, business associates, and anyone else fortunate enough to come within his orbit.

I met Al at an early stage in my life when I was considering my future academic and career prospects. I quickly discovered we had mutual interests in philosophy, science, technology, and the need to develop a better understanding of society. He took an immediate interest in discussing, exchanging, and debating views on these matters, and thus began nearly forty-five years of stimulating conversations that evolved and took on a life of their own. Al always exemplified great candor, thoughtful insight, creativity, and eloquence. When we differed, it was always done with mutual respect and constructive feedback.

In his conversations with others, Al's primary interest was to hear and understand their views. Although he may have tried to bring you around to his way of thinking, he did not get caught up in keeping score regarding the ownership of ideas that may have emerged from the discussion. Over the years, I became aware of this trait due to our mutual inability to remember who had started a particular conversation and which one of us had made which contributions toward any consensus we might reach. This was particularly poignant and ironic coming from a man who put intellectual property at the center of his thinking and teaching about property rights.

Al's interest in intellectual property was clear from the beginning of our interactions, as he evidenced a passion for innovations to solve technical and social problems. He once told me, as I pondered applying to law schools, "The only attorneys I have any use for are patent attorneys." Eventually I became his patent attorney and learned about niche areas of science and technology beyond my imagined capabilities. For that I credit his exemplary skills as a teacher.

Al's innovations were intended to make a practical difference in people's lives. He had no tolerance for ivory tower or idealistic solutions that, in his words, "didn't make any history." He also saw the danger in strident beliefs or ideologies that were promoted with a sense of certainty. On the other hand, he never let his natural skepticism about certainty stand in the way of his efforts to always push the boundaries of natural limitations, such as the laws of thermodynamics. He believed it was important to do the best you can at any moment and to strive to do even better next time.

On many occasions, Al met with frustration in promoting his inventions to governmental bureaucracies. He encountered NIMBYism (Not In My Back Yard) at the municipal level and absolutist constraints from regulatory authorities. He believed his inventions advanced existing approaches based on sound cost-benefit analyses, but they often did not fall within the narrow requirements of bureaucrats who let the perfect get in the way of the good.

Al had a strong interest in the scientific method and its application to a better understanding of society. He was passionate about how to develop "an authentic natural science of society" that utilized the scientific method but addressed the peculiarities of its subject matter: human society. Here he was encouraged by his dear friend Spencer MacCallum and his groundbreaking work on proprietary community. Both Al and Spencer were inspired by, and sought to build upon, the work done by Spencer's grandfather, Spencer Heath, on the idea of a naturalistic, humane science of society.

Al was a great proponent of markets and property rights. However, his views on property rights were not always within the ideological boundaries of many of his libertarian colleagues. His views owe a debt to the creative work of Spencer Heath, who saw property as a social creation, not subject to varied ideological or theological underpinnings. Al greatly advanced the discussion of this subject, and he has left us with a strong legacy to address a very complex aspect of social organization.

I was introduced to West Coast jazz by Al, who had a particular passion for contrapuntal jazz recordings. His musical tastes matched his own creative style. He was an improvisational thinker. He would take an interest in someone else's ideas and improvise on them, staying true to their original theme and structure but embellishing them in ways that would steer them in new, complementary directions.

Some people have the impression that Al was an atheist who put science above spiritual matters. But he had affinities with pantheism, which equates God with nature. Although he was a secular Jew, he spoke proudly about the translation of the Hebrew word *Israel*, which means "wrestles with God." In Al's view, to be a Jew meant to be someone who wrestles with nature. Like Einstein, Al felt that scientific understanding was a spiritual calling and a celebration of something transcendent.

This biography will provide you with rich insight into the breadth and depth of Al's character and capabilities. For those who knew Al well, I expect it will be a warm and poignant remembrance. For those who are just coming to know of this warm and wise man, it should be an enlightening and enriching experience.

—Bruce Canter, JD, independent legal consultant

ACKNOWLEDGMENTS

Like many biographers, I never got to meet my subject. We had some brief contact when I asked him to write the foreword to the biography I did about his best friend, Spencer MacCallum. After that there was talk of doing a similar book about him, but his health and ultimate death didn't allow him to participate, except posthumously. Al's daughter, Rosamina (Rosie), with the support of a group of Al's cohorts, called the Autonomists, committed to see this book come about.

I am indebted to Al's family and friends for their collaboration. These include siblings Jan Horn and Bettie Baer; children Rosie Lowi and Alvin Lowi III; extended family Anna Lowi, Dan Ferguson, Jason Lowi, and Leslie Cosby; and friends Jeff Solomon, Bruce Canter, Paul Mullen, Chris Boehr, John Goode, John Imig, Peter Bos, Chas Holloway, and Sara Taft. Some family and friends spoke of Alvin from beyond the grave, having preceded him in death: Ted Lowi, David Lowi, Spencer MacCallum, Jay Snelson, Chuck Estes, Harry Browne, and others.

The most important contributor was Al himself. More than half this book is his own words. They reveal the thoughts, feelings, and interests that prompted the choices and actions of his life, which is a large part of what a biography should do. As Mark Twain once wrote, "An autobiography that leaves out the little things and enumerates only the big ones is no proper picture of the man's life at all; his life consists of his feelings and his interests, with here and there an incident apparently big or little to hang the feelings on."[1]

INTRODUCTION

I first contacted Alvin while doing research for my book on Spencer MacCallum, for which Alvin wrote the foreword. The two were best friends and intellectual soulmates. They invested in each other's lives and business ventures for many years. After Spencer's passing in 2020, there was talk of doing a similar biography of Alvin. While he freely shared his ideas and insights in what could be compiled into several books, he was indifferent about a biography, preferring to leave that to others if they thought it worthwhile.

They did.

Alvin's daughter, Rosamina, and other family and friends raised the funds and provided much of the material from which this book has been crafted. The challenge was never finding material but filtering and filing it down into an accurate portrayal. Abridging more than nine decades into a few hundred pages requires leaving out so much of the good stuff, but enough remains to capture the essence of the man.

This book is part biography and part autobiography. Wherever possible it features Alvin's recollections in his own words. He was a gifted writer and skilled communicator. It is informed by those who knew him intimately and written to introduce him to those who never met him or read any of his scientific or political pieces.

Part One is a short biography tracing Alvin's ninety-two-year journey from Gadsden, Alabama (1929), to Rancho Palos Verdes, California (2021). The son of southern Jewish Democrats, he was the apple that rolled farthest from the family tree, geographically and politically. The U.S. Navy helped pay for college and grad school and sent him to California, where he met his wife and started a family. After a few years in the aerospace industry, he set out on his own as an engineer and entrepreneur. Friendships with men such as Andrew Galambos and Spencer MacCallum expanded his thinking. Many people remember life-changing conversations with Alvin, and many more had their worldviews broadened by his writings.

Which brings us to part two.

Part Two is an Alvin Lowi Jr. Reader. It has a sampling from his collected writings on subjects as diverse as global warming and economics and as deep as "The Thermodynamic Implications of Natural Society." He was a stickler for the scientific method, which he applied to everything, even to fields where others thought it didn't belong, like sociology. Al didn't expect—or even want—people to agree with him. He just wanted them to pay attention to the science in a way that facilitated progress. What he said in his monograph, "Constructing a Science of Society," applied to everything he wrote:

By following my upcoming arguments supporting these claims, the reader will be engaged in a heuristic exercise, which is designed to facilitate the tracking of an argument, not so much to persuade as to provoke inquiry and stimulate learning. In doing so, I hope he will be encouraged to question, learn, discover, understand, and solve problems on his own by experimenting with and evaluating the effects of my provisional answers or solutions by using his own thinking and experience. This effort will acquaint him first-hand with the practice of the scientific method. There is also a chance that a theory of society will emerge to the satisfaction of a skeptical and scientifically discerning reader. In that case, progress will have been made toward accrediting an authentic theory of human society.

What comes through in Al's story is a passion for life. "If I were to sum Al up in one word," his sister Bettie said, "I would say he was passionate. He was passionate about life and work and music. He was passionate about his relationships. When he loved, he loved with his whole soul."

My life has been enriched by getting to know Al. I hope you have the same experience reading about him.

Alvin Lowi Jr, Spring 1986

PART ONE
History

Alvin Lowi Jr., circa 1982, with his beer and his blowtorch,
showing a big block, dual-fuel engine

Rocket Scientist... and More

*I am keenly aware of my personal identity, a cherished gift
from my parents. I may celebrate my individuality
more often than most. Thus, I have become known as an
incorrigible individualist and I rather enjoy the distinction.*
—Alvin Lowi Jr.

Alvin Lowi Jr. was one of the most interesting people you've probably never heard of. In addition to being an actual rocket scientist, he could be called a Renaissance man, a genius, and a polymath. These terms are synonyms with subtle distinctions.

A *Renaissance man* initially meant "a cultured man of the Renaissance who was knowledgeable, educated, or proficient in a wide range of fields."[2] The *Encyclopedia Britannica* notes that "the gifted men of the Renaissance sought to develop skills in all areas of knowledge, in physical development, in social accomplishments, and in the arts." [3] The honorific hearkens back to the great artists and innovators of the Renaissance and Enlightenment periods and conjures up the likes of

Michelangelo and Leonardo da Vinci. A modern Renaissance man (or woman) is someone with deep knowledge and expertise in a number of fields.

A *genius* is usually more focused. It's someone with "an exceptional natural capacity of intellect, especially as shown in creative and original work in science, art, music, etc."[4] "Being a genius is different than merely being supersmart," said Walter Isaacson, who has written biographies of several geniuses. "Smart people are a dime a dozen, and many of them don't amount to much. What matters is creativity, the ability to apply imagination to almost any situation."[5] Thomas Edison and Albert Einstein spring to mind.

Not all geniuses are polymaths, but many polymaths are geniuses. A *polymath* "(Greek: πολυμαθής, *polymathēs*, 'having learned much'; Latin: *homo universalis*, 'universal human') is an individual whose knowledge spans a substantial number of subjects, known to draw on complex bodies of knowledge to solve specific problems."[6] John David McKee, CEO of Ins & Outs, suggests that "a polymath is simply someone who may have one area of depth, but who has a broad range of expertise in other areas as well that they can pull from to make enlightened decisions."[7]

While all three terms could be applied to Alvin, I believe *polymath* fits best; hence, the subtitle of this book. During his more than nine decades on the planet, he acquired an encyclopedic knowledge in many disciplines and used it to innovate, invent, and inform. After college, grad school, and a stint in the navy, he worked in aerospace as a design engineer on the first commercial jet aircraft, then shifted to developing jet reaction control and power systems for ballistic missiles and spacecraft. Outside of work he pursued his PhD in engineering at UCLA, with an emphasis on irreversible thermodynamics, radiation interchange, nuclear engineering, and kinetic theory.

Concurrent Careers

In a professional life that spanned more than sixty years, Al juggled several vocations. He was an *engineer* and *entrepreneur*. Marquis Who's Who Top Engineers recognized him as a "thermodynamics expert specializing in creating novel solutions for the energy industry."[8] As an entrepreneur he started or was a principal in five companies. He was interested in technologies that could have a large-scale benefit for society, such as desalinization and fuel-efficient engines.

Al's knowledge and skills impressed the other engineers who worked with him. "Al was an engineer's engineer," said Bob Benz, owner of Benz Air Engineering. "My father, himself an accomplished mechanical engineer, told me before he passed, 'Stick close to that man; he's one of the most brilliant engineers with whom I've had the pleasure of working.'"

Lanny Trefz, owner of LTR Racing Engines, once ranked the number three race-engine builder in the country, agrees:

Al was an automotive engineer with expertise in so many other areas. We worked together on the Intercooler Project at Daeco Fuels. It was a really unique design Alvin came up with. It was an engine you could put in

a semi-truck that generated enough coolant to refriger-
ate the cargo. He built another engine that would run
without oxygen for a drone going to 70,000 feet. It ran
on one-hundred percent nitro methane. Another of his
engines that I still have was assembled for Caterpillar
called a Cam engine. It's a unique thing.

Al was a *philosopher* and a *physicist,* not by academic training but by natural inclination and acquired acumen. He always
connected these two disciplines. In his monograph "Scientific
Method," he traced the history of philosophy from Aristotle
through Bacon, Spinoza, Leibnitz, Newton, Locke, and others, to Spencer Heath, whom Al met shortly before Heath's
death. According to Al, "[Heath] described the elements of an
all-encompassing philosophy of human knowledge and experience from which he was able to outline a natural science
of society."[9]

"Al was a great physicist," observes Peter Bos, who himself
has degrees from MIT and UCLA. "He had a brilliant mind and
great understanding of thermodynamics and other concepts.
He was also a very good engineer and did work on engines
with advanced designs. And his article on global warming,
'The Green Energy Boondoggle' is very insightful." [10]

Al was an *inventor* and *author*. Nobel Prize winner Albert
von Szent-Györgyi is credited with saying, "Discovery consists of seeing what everybody has seen and thinking what
nobody has thought." Al saw and thought enough unique
things that he held more than thirty U.S. patents and had
many more inventions described in confidential disclosure

documents and technical papers. "Dad just loved technology," his son Alvin III recalls. "He loved innovating; he loved creating and demonstrating that what he created could actually work and have applications in industry."

"I think Al was one of the great thinkers and writers in the field of human interaction in society," said longtime friend John Goode. "Although he never wrote a book, his papers together would make several volumes of wonderful reading about the scientific method and many other subjects. There are just so many reasons to get to know him better by reading what he wrote. To being a great thinker and writer I would add that he was a great friend."

Natural-Born Contrarian

Alvin Jr. was the second of six children in the lively Lowi household. "If you'd been sitting around the dining room table with Al and his three brothers," his sister Bettie relates, "you would've seen the sparks fly. There was not a lot of harmony in terms of political philosophies among us, but we all admired Al for his incredible brain and the fact that he was just a genius in so many ways. He was the scientist in the family, but through some of his associations he became much more involved in political issues."

"I think Al was the smartest of the brothers," recalls his sister Jan, "and they were all very smart. He had so many different skill sets because of his intellect. He was an inventor like our father, but he moved in other directions. It was a challenge to figure out what Al was thinking. He was complicated, but people with big minds are never simple."

As his sisters attest, from his earliest years Al was a contrarian—a person who takes an opposing view, especially one who rejects the majority opinion—not so much by temperament but by conviction. He was naturally cordial but intellectually demanding. Throughout his life, he used his comprehensive knowledge, sharp wits, and fierce devotion to science to analyze and debunk many popular "truths" about everything from politics and government to climate change and global warming. His modus operandi was to put a popular belief under the microscope of the scientific method and report what he saw. He welcomed debate and argument, but disagreement had to be based on data, not dogma.

"Al demanded intellectual rigor," said his friend Paul Mullen, "but he was always willing to give you credit if you were making an honest effort. He never pulled intellectual rank. He was very patient with those willing to question their assumptions, to investigate and learn new things."

One example of Al's "genial contrarian" approach is his writing on climate change. "The Green Energy Boondoggle" is a case study in applying scientific rigor to common sense, which turns out not to be common but wrongheaded in Al's opinion: "Of all the cockamamie political schemes being foisted upon the people of this country by political activists at the present time," the article begins, "the one that vexes me the most is the so-called Green New Deal. This program, funded by the federal government ostensibly to save the environment but actually to exploit pure political opportunity, is the most expensive venture ever undertaken by the federal government other than war."[11]

So much for starting your argument on neutral ground. Al wrote with his heart as well as his head.

Al was disparaging of politics and government and sought to warn people of their nefarious evils. "Foreign enemies come and go but the U.S. Government under which Americans actually live is their life-long enemy," he once wrote. "Statecraft is a blood-sucking parasite on the taxpayers (the subjects). It is inherently collectivistic and is therefore wholly contradictory and blind to individual human life."[12]

His harsh criticism of the political system was a result of trying to make sense of it. Jeff Solomon, an admirer who is cataloging Al's writings, points out that "Al's essence was not political at all; it was scientific. He was a student of the scientific method. He believed the answers to humanity's problems would be found by applying science, with a proper epistemology, to human affairs. And in addition to the content, he wrote with a profundity and wit that indelibly stamps many of his passages with a magical eloquence worth reading over and over again."

"Alvin was of the most original and innovative thinkers of the twentieth and twenty-first centuries," said Len DeLuna, Al's son-in-law, who knew him well. "An accomplished engineer, he anticipated many of the energy and climate-related conundrums that the world now faces. He invented devices to alleviate potable water shortages and to keep seafood fresh. He came up with innovative methods to make internal combustion engines more economical, while generating electricity at the same time. But it was his social and political musings that will, perhaps, have the most lasting impact."

Egocentric Humility

Underlying all Al's accomplishments was an innate and insatiable curiosity. The knowledge he acquired thereby did not lead to hubris but to what he called "egocentric humility." In a paper written near his seventieth birthday, he gave readers a glimpse into how his mind worked:

> When I realized that my senses were little more than a peep-hole to the world at large, I became curious how the knowledge I could gain through this small window made me more aware of my ignorance. It seems I am smart enough to ask one good question regarding a certain alleged regularity of the world. Then, if I get a satisfactory answer, I become smart enough to ask two such questions, and so on *ad infinitum*. My ignorance grows in geometric ratio to my knowledge. Thus, my mind is like a balloon. It expands in size as I fill its volume with knowledge, whereupon its surface representing my exposure to ignorance expands accordingly.

"How shall I regard this dilemma?" he goes on to ask, adding:

> While I am encouraged to rely on my own faculties to bring me dependable knowledge of the world around me, I find that the more I know, the more I do not know. I may be inclined to think, "woe is me." When I awaken to the fact that this is the first day in the rest

of my life, I realize an appropriate posture for me to take for the duration of whatever remains of it is "egocentric humility." For me, this means I continue to rely on whatever potency my own intellect provides me, while remembering that I cannot know all the answers. Alas, I can't even know all the questions! But I can accept, even enjoy, my kinship with my fellow man as an equal, knowing that he, too, has a similar burden.[13]

What factors went into shaping Al's life and work? How did a Jewish boy from rural Alabama, born just three months ahead of the Great Depression, come to have such an outsized influence on thousands of people through his ideas and inventions? This short biography is a modest attempt to answer those questions.

Alvin Lowi Sr. and Janice Haas Lowi Family, circa 1947
Top left to right: Theodore, Alvin Jr.
Seated left to right: Janice, Bettie, David, Bertram, Jan, Alvin Sr.

1032 Fourth Avenue

We all wonder how we could have succeeded to maturity
and liked it without the kind of family nourishment we enjoyed.
All of us feel especially privileged thereby. Ours was
a precious inheritance which we like to celebrate on occasion
at the risk of offending our spouses, intimidating our in-laws,
embarrassing our children and boring our friends.
—Alvin Lowi Jr.

The Lowis were a Jewish family whose roots went backward from Gadsden, Alabama, through Meridian, Mississippi, and Mobile, Alabama, to Budapest, Hungary, and what was once Bohemia. Alvin Rosenbaum Lowi Sr. grew up in Meridian. After graduating from Georgia Tech in 1917 with a degree in electrical engineering, he enlisted in the Army and went to officers training camp, then served in France as part of the Signal Corps during World War I. He was a patriot who also served his country in World War II when he was in his forties.

After Alvin Sr. got out of the army, he took a job with Alabama Power Company in Gadsden, where his uncles lived.

Janice Marks Hass, a Gadsden resident, who had returned home after attending the Cincinnati Conservatory from 1924 to 1025, met and fell in love with Alvin, who was ten years her senior. Alvin courted her on the Coosa River in his boat, and they were married in 1926. The Lowis moved to 1032 Fourth Avenue after their wedding and never left.

Alvin Sr. passed away in 1975, age seventy-nine, and Janice in 1995, age eighty-nine. It was the only house the Lowi children knew growing up.

The Lowi children arrived in two batches. First came the boys: David (1927); Alvin Jr. (1929), also called Bubby or Asa but never Alvin, which was reserved for Alvin Sr.; Theodore (1931), called Ted; and Bertram (1934), called Bert. Years later they were joined by two sisters: Jan (1942) and Bettie (1944).

This book is about Al Jr., which casts the rest of the family in supporting roles. This is not to minimize their own interesting and intriguing lives; it's just the way biographies work. This memoir has been undertaken with the input of those relatives who are living and is informed by the recordings and writings of those who are no longer here.

Home Base

Every story is rooted somewhere, and Al's starts at 1032 Fourth Avenue, Gadsden, Alabama. The Lowi home was in a modest neighborhood of working-class families. "Only white families lived on our block," Al wrote in a family history, *The Lowi Family Tree, Autobiographical Annotations and Other Folklore*, "but there were black families living in the next block. The public schools for us white kids were all within short walking distances. The black kids were not as fortunate. I never did understand why they couldn't go to school with us. However, they did play with us after school on the same playgrounds in the neighborhood and some of us had the same music teachers, barbers, and doctors. To us, the blacks were our 'Schwarzes' neighbors. We were their Jewish neighbors. Neither we nor our black neighbors took the rest of the neighborhood for granted. It was a peaceful and civil arrangement but we generally understood the rest of the community believed they were destined for a heaven that would not admit us. As far as we were concerned, they could have it that way."

The original house only had two bedrooms. Janice's grand piano occupied one, where she taught lessons to white and black students alike. A room was added in 1935 that became the boys' dormitory. David and Al got the twin beds; Ted and Bert got the homemade, double-deck bunk bed. Age had its privileges. "Each of us had one drawer in a single chest-of-drawers where we kept all our private property," Al wrote. "We shared a single clothes-closet and bathroom with our parents."

At no time did the entire family—six children and two parents—live under the same roof. When the next baby was born, the eldest sibling would move out to the living room. When one of his sisters was born, Bert moved in with his grandparents to make room for the baby. Janice's parents, Isaac and Fedora (Maw Maw), lived just around the corner and provided a second home for the kids.

"Dad was the head of the house," said Bettie, the youngest child. "He was loud and demanding. A retired army major, he was extremely patriotic. If you asked him who he was, he would say, 'First, I'm an American. Second, I'm an Alabamian. Third, I'm a Jew.' He was at the Huntsville Arsenal during World War II, so the boys took care of Mother. They did everything to help her. My oldest brother drove her to the hospital when I was born in 1944 because Dad wasn't home. When he did come home from the army, he had suffered some kind of breakdown. He was fragile and would have outbursts that were a little scary."

Jan, a few years older than Bettie, adds more details. "Dad had been in the army in the First and Second World Wars. Unfortunately, he was stationed at the Huntsville Arsenal, where they made chemical bombs. He was very patriotic and would never have spoken up in any way, but he didn't believe in what he was doing, and he had a nervous breakdown. He was put in a hospital and had spinal taps, I think it was. It really affected him, and he would have what Mother called 'spells.' He had a rough time of it but he did recover. He got his strength back and lived a long time after that."

"Our mom was the rock in our family," Bettie recalls. "She was tiny, barely five feet. She had this beautiful soul and everyone idolized her, my brothers especially. She was their queen. She was the center of their lives until they married. She was strong but not particularly assertive. She was extremely bright."

"It is inconceivable how any of us could have persevered in our lives as we have without her support and inspiration," Al noted. "Not that she was ever a companion-in-arms or that we ever manifested her most ardent wishes. (She dreamed I would become a concert violinist like Yehudi Menuhin.) She simply accepted us, contrariness and all, and never wavered in her devotion and loyalty to each of us. From Mother, we learned to experience beauty and to accept ourselves as a part of that experience."

At the core of Janice's character was her faith. "My grandmother was a pillar of the temple where we were active members," said David's daughter, Leslie Cosby. "As everybody grew up and left, not many married within the faith, but it was a strong part of our growing up. My grandmother was at temple every Friday night until she couldn't do it anymore. My grandfather didn't go very much. He was not a very religious person, but he supported my grandmother as she held the temple together."

"We were Jewish but we were warned by my father that we shouldn't wear our Jewishness on our sleeves," Jan said. "He didn't think it was safe to talk about being Jewish in Gadsden, a predominantly Southern Baptist community. Our family for generations past had been religious, but my dad didn't believe in organized religion, even though he went to temple with Mother because she wanted him to. Mother was always there. She was president of the sisterhood and kept the temple open. The boys wouldn't deny being Jewish, but none of them really practiced their Judaism as adults."

After the boys were gone, the Gadsden Temple was the target of a firebombing on March 26, 1960, in which Alvin Sr. made the headlines. As reported by WBRC Fox6 News:

Alvin Lowi went through World War I and World War II without a single bullet wound, only to get shot in the hand outside his temple on a Friday night in Gadsden.

His granddaughter, Leslie Cosby, recalls the role her grandfather played, trying to help the other man shot, Alan Cohn, a man who survived a bullet to his heart.

The two men had been shot just after Molotov cocktails were thrown through stained glass windows of Congregation Beth Israel on Gadsden's Chestnut Street. . . .

Local historian Danny Crownover says Rabbi Rubin urged the panicked congregation to stay inside as Lowi and Cohn ran outside to catch the assailant. They found themselves face to face with Hubert Jackson Jr. who also went by the name Jerry Hunt.[14]

Hunt, a Nazi sympathizer, was arrested and later died in a car accident. Cohn survived after receiving twenty pints of blood. Alvin Sr. carried that bullet in his hand for the rest of his life. Apparently, it was in a bad position to have it removed without compromising the eventual use of his hand.

Bettie, who was there with her family, recalls: "David was the one who discovered the entrance of the bullet that had entered Alan's side, not his heart. He directed the emergency crew to the origin of the blood loss, which saved Alan's life. I distinctly remember that. I also remember that Ted, and perhaps Bert, read about the bombing the following morning in the New York Times, which reported it as an anti-Semitic attack. But we all felt it was an isolated attack by a disgruntled and misinformed teenager. It was quite upsetting for the community, as the service was actually the dedication of a new addition to the temple, and on the dais alongside Rabbi Rubin were two or three Protestant ministers."

Music, Education, Table Talk

The Lowi family was very musical. "Mom had one year at Cincinnati Conservatory before her family ran out of money," Bettie shares. "She taught piano lessons in our home and was also the most sought-after church organist in town. She played organ at the temple for more than sixty years."

Each of Janice's children was required to play an instrument. David played the clarinet and then oboe in the Gadsden High School Band. He loved all music, especially jazz. Al took up the violin but didn't want to be seen with the instrument. He made his mother carry it in public. Ted played the oboe and Bert the bassoon because that's what the band director at school needed them to play. Ted got good enough to win a scholarship to Michigan State University, and Bert played bassoon at Duke.

The boys sang together as the Lowi Brothers Quartet in the late 1930s and early '40s, with their mother accompanying them on piano. "When I was about four years old," Bert recalls, "my mother had the bright idea to team me up with my brothers into the Lowi Brothers Barbershop Quartet to perform—with some notoriety—at various venues in north Alabama. I ate it up, but my brothers, not so much, and when my oldest brother's voice began to change, that spelled the end of the quartet and I was just another kid on the block. But that's when I began the process of trying to BE like them—the very talented individuals they turned out to be—with emphasis on the words 'talented' and individuals.'"

That talent was honed by education, which was also paramount to the Lowis. "My dad would say the most important thing to him was that his children be educated," Bettie explains. "All six of us got university educations, and five of us earned advanced degrees. All my brothers were amazing students. Al, as brilliant as he was, was not the best student in the family because he was easily distracted. His head was always a little bit in the clouds."

Decades later, Al's daughter, Rosie, noted the same tendency. "My dad had a very curious nature. His brain was always in the clouds. He always seemed to be in his own world. These are descriptions I've heard my aunts and uncles give of my dad. He was exasperating because he wouldn't pay attention; he was focusing on something else. He got the bulk of my grandfather's discipline because he seemed uncooperative. But in fact he was just not paying attention."

But Al wasn't some moody, detached loner; he was the life of the party! "I remember all of Al's friends would hang out at the house," Jan recalls. "He was quite a ringleader, with lots of close friends. He played football and always had a girlfriend. He was very handsome and popular."

After high school, when the brothers started leaving home, joining the military was a good bet. "David joined the army, and Al and Bert joined the Navy ROTC program to help pay for college," Jan said. "Ted wanted to join but he got very sick. When he came home from the hospital in New Orleans, they didn't know if he was going to pull through. He spent months in bed, reading. I remember Mother would go to the library and check out stacks of books. That's when he became the real student he always was after that."

Ted's daughter, Anna, elaborates. "Dad had a scholarship to Tulane, but he got sick in his senior year of high school and freshman year of college. He was very ill with ulcerative colitis and really ought to have died. At that time he actually got closer to his brothers. They visited a lot and brought him books. He read everything he could get his hands on. He got a music scholarship to Michigan State and graduated in record time. He was determined to get on with his life and his career, and he never looked back."

The central piece of furniture in the Lowi household was the dining room table. (This would also one day be the case at 2146 Toscanini Drive in San Pedro, California, Al Jr.'s home for sixty years.) "Food and hospitality have always been at the center of our family's tradition and vitality," Bettie wrote in the Lowi family cookbook. "Among the warmest memories is dinnertime at the Lowi house on Fourth Avenue in Gadsden, Alabama. Our mother tended to the dinner time menu as a dedicated wife and mother was expected to do in those days. Although there was always a black housekeeper/cook around the house, Mother was ultimately the manager of the kitchen and dinner table, which was always crowded and boisterous. There was always room at our table for one more mouth. Anyone who happened to drop by around mealtime was cordially and heartily welcomed to pull up a chair."

The table was also the setting for heated family arguments, Al Jr. often serving as the catalyst. "He was a little far out for the rest of us," Bettie said. "He was a philosopher in so many ways and very committed to his thoughts, which created such tension among his brothers. I don't know that any of us in the family completely understood his philosophy."

Al and Ted were the leading protagonists in these debates. Reflecting back on these times, Al wrote of himself in the third person in his *Lowi Family Tree*:

> Anyone who can bear listening to Al expound on politics and government will recognize that he is looking over his shoulder anticipating an argument from someone somewhere sitting in judgment. Ordinarily, one would think this person would be his father. That would be true to some extent. But the more prominent "someone" in this case would be his younger brother (Dr. Theodore Lowi). Ted acknowledged his longstanding arguments with Al in his most acclaimed book (*The End of Liberalism*, W. W. Norton, 1969) and how those arguments (actually a family tradition) had significance for him, albeit at the expense of his vocal cords. No doubt, those arguments brought out some of Ted's best teachings and writings, but they were also provocations for Al's interest in and study of the broader aspects of natural history in an effort to look after his sanity. Al always knew he had no hope of winning the argument.

Even many years later, Ted and Al's niece, Leslie, witnessed the same passionate disputes. "When Al would come back to my grandparents' house and discuss things he was interested in, there could be some scary moments because he was different from my grandfather. He had ideas that didn't fit the mold of small-town Alabama. The brothers would argue and discuss and sometimes scream at each other. An outsider would've been a bit set back because it seemed like they were really mad, but they were just having discussions."

Senior and Junior

"You always had your own agenda," brother Bert told Al on a family Zoom call in 2021. "You were doing things on your own long before the rest of us were. That's why you had trouble with Dad, because you weren't a dutiful son."

"Well, Dad misunderstood me that way, you see," Al countered. "I had a deep attention span for everything he was doing, but I didn't seem to come to attention whenever he barked it out. I was not a good soldier. But I followed Dad around a lot. He couldn't shake me. I was like a puppy. I hung out with him to learn the tools of the trade. He was a good craftsman. He was very versatile. He could use about every hand tool ever been made. He was not too keen on disciplinary methods, though. He did it army style. He would frequently slap me with the back of his hand on the impulse that I did something wrong, which I usually did. I was already a target. Maybe because I was named after him, he expected more. He was pretty spontaneous when it came to discipline. It was the apologies that would come afterward that were memorable. His discipline always hurt him more than it did me. He suffered more from a slap than I did. I came to appreciate that and to have great sympathy for him.

"I never could keep in step, but I learned a hell of a lot from him, even though his manner of going about his business was not very instructive. I learned by watching and doing. He enjoyed the company, and so it was a good arrangement. I had a really good relationship with my father. I'd rather that is what's remembered instead of the slaps and other discipline I got."

In *The Lowi Family Tree*, Al shared more of the good memories he had of his dad—like this one:

I remember being about five or six years old and sitting on Dad's lap in the rocking chair while he studied the *U.S. Pharmacopeia*. It was a dictionary of formulas about the size of the *Oxford Unabridged Dictionary*. You needed a wheelbarrow to move it. He would sit in his chair in the living room every night and read up on one or more formulas. He lived in that damn book. The pictures and drawings were interesting to me.

Dad would get these ideas and write them down and experiment with the formula. He'd go out and buy the chemicals and experiment. Some of his creations included headache powder, hair oil, bleach, and even an artificial sweetener. He would solubilize saccharine since we couldn't get sugar during the war and we'd have it on the table with an eye dropper. This was years before other sweeteners came out. If he'd taken it a little further, we'd be gazillionaires now, but he'd get bored with whatever and go off and make something else. He did the same thing with his bleach before there was Clorox.

"Dad had strong opinions about almost everything," Al added. "He never cared much for comparative philosophy and cared even less whether his own primitive philosophy agreed with the 'sages.' He was a rabid anti-communist, committing his last act of corporal punishment on [me] to show his disapproval of fooling around with the Marxist notions [I] had brought home from school [Georgia Tech]. Right or wrong, Dad was so consistent that we never had to suffer any confusion as to who he was, what he stood for and what we were to him, which we knew to be a lot, notwithstanding keen sibling rivalry and stern discipline."

▼

The Lowis had been in America about a century when Al Jr. and his siblings were born (1927–1944). They valued and carried on many of the family traditions, but they also grew wings and flew a fair distance from the family tree, especially Al Jr. He was an outlier—someone who stands apart from others of his or her group. Yet he was also fiercely loyal to his family, as were his brothers and sisters, despite their obvious differences.

Al would wholeheartedly agree with Elizabeth Berg, best-selling author of *Family Traditions* and *Open House*, who wrote, "You are born into your family and your family is born into you. No returns. No exchanges."[15] To which Al would add the words that opened this chapter, "All of us feel especially privileged thereby. Ours was a precious inher-itance which we like to celebrate on occasion at the risk of offending our spouses, intimidating our in-laws, embarrassing our children and boring our friends."

It's also an inheritance they would all enrich during their long lifetimes and pass along as a legacy to others.

Alvin Jr. doing drone work near Korea in 1953

CHAPTER 3

The Wider World

Leave the door open and see who walks in!
—Alvin Lowi Jr.

After high school, David Lowi went to Georgia Tech, his dad's alma mater. Al followed him a year later. David studied chemical engineering; Al pursued a degree in mechanical engineering. He also signed up for Navy ROTC to help pay for college.

Thinking back on their time at Tech, Al said, "It's amazing David and I made it through. At one point I got kicked out of the dormitory because it was only for freshman and I'd become a sophomore. We loaded in with cousin Fay Greil and her husband, Gaston. We slept in one bed, for God's sake. It was a hardship. We had to catch the bus really early to make it to class. But they put up with us, and we learned quite a bit from being paying guests. Then we moved in with Billy Singleton. His family had a big house, and we each had our own bed. David and I moved all over the place. We could have written a book about how to survive in academia without a roof over your head."

In addition to his itinerant lifestyle and active social life, Al had a full schedule of classes and Navy ROTC duties. And he was the wingman for his older brother. "Dad was extremely close to his eldest brother, David," Al's daughter Rosie recalls. "They went to the same high school and college. They shared a room at Georgia Tech and had all the adventures of students on a very limited budget. They built cars together and even had the same girlfriends. After college, David stayed in Gadsden and ran the family business, a chemical company, which his son-in-law still runs. It broke my dad's heart when we lost his brothers David in 2015 and Ted in 2017."

San Diego and Atlanta

As part of his navy commitment, Al served as a midshipman on the USS *Iowa* in 1948 while enrolled at Georgia Tech. Commissioned as an ensign, he served as an engineering officer on steam and diesel vessels in the Pacific Fleet Amphibious Forces during the Korean War. He participated in, and was decorated for, the amphibious assault on Inchon in 1950. Upon returning to school and graduating in 1951, he went to San Diego, his next duty station, where he was officer-in-charge of the Assault Boat Engineers School at the Naval Amphibious Base Coronado. He also directed an experimental assault boat development project for the Navy Bureau of Ships.

"While stationed in California, Al discovered West Coast jazz, with its freedom of expression within its own rules of engagement," his brother Bert said. "And he brought that home to me. But the navy was the real hook. Of course, I had vaguely known our uncle Ralph Haas, a Naval Academy graduate killed in action on Iwo Jima. But he was a bona fide hero to my oldest brothers, which no doubt played a part in Al's signing up for NROTC at Georgia Tech. Hearing about his midshipman cruises and knowing that the navy was paying for all this—including some of his college expenses—I was determined to follow suit when my time came. Which I did, and it was fateful.

"Al's navy service gave him real-life experience in engineering propulsion systems," Bert added, "something that probably figured into his going to work in civilian life for the TRW Aerospace Corp working on spacecraft propulsion. Mine took me on a parallel path that I never could have dreamed of. Stationed at the Naval Aerospace Crew Equipment Lab, I helped train the original *Mercury 7* astronauts in using the full pressure 'space' suits developed by the laboratory I was working at. Finally we were on the same team, except that I outranked him on the navy side, so we got a couple of laughs out of that."

During his time in San Diego, Al fell in love with and married Guillermina (Mina) Gerardo Alvarez in 1953. Their son Alvin III tells the story. "When Dad was in the Navy, he got stationed in San Diego, where he met my mother. She was working in the U.S. but didn't speak English. She was divorced and had a young son. It was not long after they met that they went to Yuma and got married in May of 1953. They were together for fifty-nine years until her death in 2012.

"Dad grew up in the South in a traditionally Jewish family in a small town in Alabama," Alvin said. "Now imagine, a traditional Jewish family from the South dealing with their son running off and marrying a Mexican citizen who had been married, divorced, and had a small boy [whom Al later adopted]. Her entire family lived in Mexico. Putting these two starkly different families together through marriage was a very challenging undertaking, but my dad was fearless about this. He loved my mom dearly and worked hard at getting to know her family, their culture, their traditions, their food, even their dances. He loved the music. It was just amazing how he respected and accepted it all."

"My dad embraced my mother's family," Rosie confirms. "He embraced the Mexican culture. He tried to learn Spanish. He was very open-minded toward other cultures. He loved his Mexican in-laws. My uncle Pancho was the mayor of Tijuana in 1965. He was married to my mother's youngest sister. Dad and Uncle Pancho were really great friends; they even invested in each other's projects."

Al and Mina moved to Atlanta in 1954, where Al began postgraduate study at Georgia Tech. While there, he also taught at the Woodruff School of Mechanical Engineering and did research in the effects of acoustic resonance on natural convection heat transfer. The Lowis spent any free time they had in Gadsden with Al's family. "My aunts have stories about the huge impact Mina had on the Gadsden community," Rosie said. "She was so exotic; no one in Gadsden had ever met anyone from Mexico before. She was all adventure for them. They loved her, her language, her culture."

Los Angeles

Al earned his master's in mechanical engineering in 1956, got his Navy discharge, and the Lowis headed for greater

Los Angeles. He took a job as a design engineer for Garrett Corporation. Two years later he went to work for Ramo-Wooldridge. His career in aerospace and beyond is detailed in the next chapter.

Al loved his roots in the South, but California was a better fit for his thinking and temperament. "My folks would've liked to live in San Diego," said Rosie, "but in the 1950s, the aerospace industry in Los Angeles was beginning to boom. That's where the work was, so they moved to the Los Angeles area and found an apartment in Inglewood. My mom often talked about this because she was pregnant with my sister Edna, and the apartment was upstairs and she couldn't take going up and down the stairs with me as a toddler. And my half brother David, who is six years older than me, was with us. So, Mom convinced Dad to buy a little house in Torrance. It was a brand-new ticky-tacky box where we lived until 1962 when they bought the house in San Pedro, which was incorporated into Rancho Palos Verdes in 1973. Dad lived there until he passed away in 2021."

It was a busy household.

"Al and Mina's was the neighborhood hot spot," remembers their niece Anna. "Everyone gathered at their house. Not only was it a blast to be there, but Al and Mina were phenomenal cooks who loved to share what they made. There was always something going on, and Al just loved to be part of it. He could find a way of having a meaningful conversation with anyone. He took what you said very seriously, and it had nothing to do with how old you were or how well-read you might have been. He was eager to draw you out and hear from you. There was this urgency about making a connection with whomever he was speaking with. I remember as a high school student, he was one of the only grown-ups who really listened and who was really interested in those little things that worried me so much as a fourteen-year-old."

That focus and connection also made Al a danger on the roads, as Anna knew firsthand. "I remember being a passenger with some frequency in his diesel Mercedes, the one he was always tinkering with. It was terrifying! We'd be hurtling along the highway at eighty-five miles an hour, and I tried not to have a conversation with him because he looks you straight in the face. One time I was trying to put my seat belt on, and he said, 'Oh, don't bother with the seat belt. It's never worked.' We were in a minor accident once when he picked us up at the airport. My dad (Ted) was in the back seat, and Al turned around to talk to him like they were chatting at the kitchen table. He drove right into a pole in the parking garage of LAX!"

The Lowis loved socializing. They also did whatever they could to encourage young people, whether they were family, friends, or strangers. Alvin III said, "Mom and Dad opened our house to extended family and friends throughout the years as far back as I can remember, all the way until near the end of Dad's life. They once took in a friend of mine who got sideways with his stepdad and was thrown out of his house. He lived with us while I was finishing high school. There were others who spent time at our house, like Bruce Canter, one of Dad's myriad 'extended sons.' He lived with us for more than two years while getting his law degree."

"Rosie and I met in England at Reading University," Bruce recounts. "After graduating, I decided to come west to California. I stopped by to visit Rosie and met Al. I ended up living with the Lowis and getting very close to Al. I had a background in philosophy and was very interested in politics. We had lots of discussions over the years, and he had a large influence on me and my development. I went on to become an attorney. I even became Al's patent attorney for a time. I remember Al saying, 'The only attorneys I have any use for are patent attorneys.'"

Family Life

Like many families, the Lowis had their challenges. "There were strains throughout the years because my mother developed some bipolar issues that went undiagnosed," Alvin III explains. "It showed up in her abuse of alcohol and prescription drugs. These grossly altered her personality, especially in the evenings. She went from a certain person during the day, when she was sober, and turned into somebody else on the alcohol and the pills. Needless to say, that created a difficult situation and tumultuous relationship. Dad managed it the best way he could. They had four kids, and he refused to break up the family. He would not leave Mom or divorce her. He just wouldn't do it."

"My mom was an extremely jealous woman," Alvin adds. "It did not take much for her to go off. Maybe that was PTSD from her first husband, who was, I've heard, quite the womanizer. Maybe that's why. And when she found out that Dad had dated my aunt Jean before my uncle David married her, that was an issue for Mom. It definitely created some outbursts at family gatherings."

Al's sister, Bettie, provides some pertinent background. "Al and Jean were in the same class at Gadsden High School, where they had been a couple. Al joined the navy, and Jean wanted to marry him before he left. When he didn't agree, she married someone else, who, unfortunately, was killed in an accident shortly thereafter. Then Jean married big brother David. There were tensions in Al and Mina's home over this, but our family shares a positive approach to life. We don't suffer from depression. Al always handled things like this in a positive way."

"Al dated Jean before Dave married her," his sister Jan said. "Jean was one of the few good-looking Jewish girls they grew up with. She got married after high school, but they were in a terrible accident and her husband died. Mother made my brothers go visit her while she was recovering, and David wound up marrying her. When Al married Mina, she was jealous of Jean, but there was no reason for it. She would've been jealous of anybody Al had loved."

In later life, Al made a space for himself that served as office and refuge. "In the early 1990s, my dad built an addition on the house as a workspace for his professional life as a freelancer," Rosie said. "It included workstations, an area to meet with clients, drafting tables, a wet bar for entertaining, a bedroom, a bathroom, and loads of decking and windows to make the most of the beautiful views from the top of the house. My mother called it his 'conuco,' which was her slang for 'slave quarters.'[16] Actually, it was a joke. She *refused* to climb those stairs. There were two phone lines in the house—this was before cell phones. Mom would call Dad on his line when she wanted to talk or ask him something. We always found that hilarious. She would even leave him messages on his answering machine.

"What was remarkable about Dad was how productive he managed to be in spite of the challenges, stresses, and emotional crises that happened at home," Rosie went on to say. "He was able to focus on his work—creatively and innovatively—and at the same time be engaged with his family and extended family. Music was also a big part of our lives at home. We children played musical instruments; we had family concerts. It was joyful."

"Al was brilliant, but there were emotional areas where he was not as tuned in," said friend and confidante Sara Taft. "We talked about this, and he agreed. He had issues with his wife that he didn't know how to deal with. Being trained as a therapist, I would fill him in on things he could do. Sometimes it worked; sometimes it didn't. His wife was extremely volatile. He used to say he never knew when a thrown plate might be going to hit him. He spent a lot of time in his office to escape emotional harassment. I'm impressed he got as much done as he did. Al didn't let opposition stop him. Even though he was hampered by his marriage, it didn't stop him from doing what he was doing. A lot of people would have quit if they had to live with what he did. Yet, he was devoted to his family; they were a real priority with him."

⌄

Al was an adoring husband and father. But he was also both a military veteran and a congenial anarchist. He proudly

served his county at home and abroad, yet he roundly criti-
cized its government and abstained from politics. He was also
an aerospace engineer and an intrepid entrepreneur who left
a comfortable career inside the military-industrial complex
because of its bent toward weaponization and launched out
on his own. The next chapter traces where his ideas and inventions took him.

Alvin Jr. with his "Sea Chill" unit, circa late 1970s
This unit would suck in sea water and chill it to a frozen slush,
then pump it over fish in the hold

CHAPTER 4

Engineer and Entrepreneur

If that's your concern, here's the solution.
—Alvin Lowi Jr.

After Al had earned his master's degree in mechanical engineering from Georgia Tech, he and Mina moved to the Los Angeles area, the hub of the burgeoning aerospace industry, in 1956. He was soon hired by the AiResearch Division of Garrett Corp. He worked as a design engineer on the first commercial jet aircraft, his focus on systems dealing with cabin pressure, air conditioning, heat exchangers, and auxiliary power. In 1958 Al took a position at Ramo-Wooldridge, which became TRW Space Technology Laboratories. He helped develop power systems for ballistic missiles and spacecraft. Two years later he joined the technical staff of Aerospace Corporation in El Segundo.

Al's brother Bert was in the navy and stationed in California while Al was there. Bert had a master's degree in psychology, and at one point the two brothers worked together on space-related projects for NASA before it was NASA. John Fowler, a fellow graduate from Georgia Tech and Al's lifelong friend, also came to California and worked in aerospace. In time, John would mentor Al's son, Alvin III, when he first joined Hughes Aircraft.

Al had a habit of forming deep friendships with smart people, many of whom were engineers he met at work, like Andrew Galambos and Don Allen. There were also engineers and scientists Al met through the Free Enterprise Institute, like Chris Boehr, Jeff Solomon, and John Imig. He would meet and befriend still others, like Bob Benz and Lanny Trefz, when he consulted or ran his own businesses.

Private Practice

Al left Aerospace Corporation in 1966 to pursue his own consulting and business ventures, which he did for the next fifty-five years until his death. Marquis Who's Who Top Engineers gives a brief overview of Al's career accomplishments:

> Dr. Lowi was a member of the technical staff of Aerospace Corporation, where he would remain until 1966, when he became the principal of Alvin Lowi and Associates. Between 1968 and 1976, Dr. Lowi was also the President of Terraqua, Inc. He took over as Vice President of Daeco Fuels and Engineering Co. in 1978, a position he held until 1990, when he became President of Lion Engineering, Inc., a firm that has collaborated on propulsion systems and engine solutions for NASA, among other projects. In addition to his work in indus-

try, Dr. Lowi has been a visiting research professor at the University of Pennsylvania and a senior lecturer for the Free Enterprise Institute. He has contributed extensively to professional journals and holds more than 30 patents for devices catalogued in the book "The Patent Estate of Alvin Lowi Jr."[17]

The Marquis piece also states, "Dr. Lowi was awarded his Doctor of Philosophy in engineering by the University of California, Los Angeles," but this was an error. "Dad completed the work for his doctorate in 1961 but never received his degree due to unforeseen circumstances," Rosie explained. "At the last minute, the engineering department rejected his choice of languages to satisfy the languages requirement. He had selected Russian and Spanish, and UCLA demanded one of the languages had to be either French or German. Then his dissertation adviser committed suicide just before he signed off on Dad's dissertation. So, even though he never 'walked' and received his degree, he did complete all the work and UCLA did recognize him as an alumnus."

A more intimate account of Al's career comes from his son Alvin III, who followed his dad into engineering and aerospace. As a student engineer, Alvin III worked with his dad at Daeco Fuels and Engineering in the late 1970s before completing his degree at Cornell. When Alvin III moved back to California, he consulted with his father on several projects.

"Dad started Alvin Lowi Jr. and Associates in 1966, and it functioned until his death in 2021," Alvin III said. "His work developing technologies and products resulted in several domestic and foreign patents. He had other businesses and ventures as well, such as Terraqua, which he started in 1968. Based in San Pedro, California, it was built on patents he developed and worked on for a few years after he left the aerospace industry. One product was a desktop water purification unit designed for residential use, called Quench. Another was a device called Sea Chill, designed for fishermen to allow them to freeze sea water in order to keep fish cold when they were on extended trips." (More about this company later in the chapter.)

"In 1978, my dad became vice president of Daeco Fuels and Engineering in Wilmington, California, and was with them until 1990. He went in principally as a result of consulting work he did earlier for Daeco and some of their clients. This got him involved in the racing domain. For example, he did consulting for Dan Gurney and the Toyota racing teams because they were burning up their turbocharged engines. Dad designed an inner cooling system for them; that was a very successful project.

"Dad started Lion Engineering in 1990. The impetus for the company was an engine design he patented that was made to be a power plant for high-altitude, unmanned aircraft. This was part of a NASA mission to fly over the polar caps. I had a suspicion that NASA was secretly working with DoD—Department of Defense. That aircraft mission was the precursor to the drones now used in military applications. Dad won a phase one contract to develop the engine based on his patents, which then led to a phase two contract that produced some groundbreaking technology. Dad started to apply for a phase three contract, which would've allowed seed money to flow in from NASA and other government agencies so he could partner with a manufacturer to make a commercial version of the engine. But NASA decided to shift the direction of the drone project, so that was the end of that.

"Then there was Motiv Engines," Alvin went on. "Dad was their principal design and development engineer. Motiv Engines produced a compact, single-cylinder engine that generated a lot of output for its size. In addition to all his projects, consulting, and business ventures, Dad was also a forensic consultant. He was used by a company called Impact General that dealt with forensic issues involving litigation. I helped him on several cases up until the point where I got my professional engineering license in 1991. By then, Dad, didn't want to do that work anymore, so he started referring his clients to me. That's how I got started in the industry, which led to the company I'm now a partner in, called Collision and Injury Dynamics. So, in a roundabout way, he spawned an entire career path for me.

"When you look back at Terraqua, Daeco Fuels, and his other business ventures," concluded Alvin, "Dad was extremely generous with his time and technology, but he wasn't necessarily the best judge of character. This led to some tragic situations that interrupted his ability to do the things he wanted to do. That's what ultimately happened with Terraqua. He had to sell a majority stake in order to continue funding the company, and that's when the investors were able to take control. They eventually ran the company into the ground. There are people who have business acumen and who find venture capital firms that want to invest in new technology. That's where Dad relied on other people, and unfortunately they were not as scrupulous as he'd hoped.

"Dad could have been a very wealthy man based on his expertise and patents. He had a genuinely golden heart, and he trusted people too willingly. Yet while he was not a wealthy man, monetarily speaking, he felt wealthy in terms of the things he was able to accomplish and the love he shared with his extended family. Dad really didn't care that much about money."

Bruce Canter, Al Jr.'s friend and onetime patent attorney, agrees. "Al was very trusting and not a savvy businessman like his son. I often thought that if Alvin III had been older and able to counsel his father in business, some of the earlier pitfalls might have been avoided."

Based on extensive research, Walter Isaacson, former managing editor of *Time* magazine and president of the Aspen Institute, declared: "Innovation requires having at least three things: a great idea, the engineering talent to execute it, and the business savvy (plus deal-making moxie) to turn it into a successful product."[18]

Al had two of the three components it takes to be a successful innovator.

Terraqua

Al poured his mind and heart into Terraqua, so it bears a more in-depth look. He had worked on desalination while in the navy, and he continued to develop his ideas as a civilian.

"In the late 1960s, I had a metal fabrication business, and Al contacted me about making parts for Terraqua," recalls John Imig, owner of Imig Industries. "Al was good at finding ways to do things without spending a fortune. For instance, he figured out how to use an electric heater made for coffeepots in the Quench machine, which was a home desalination unit. He was good at everything: scientific theory, physics, mechanical and electrical engineering. He was also good at social science matters."

Al's best friend, Spencer MacCallum, was also part of Terraqua. "Spencer gave Terraqua its name, vision, and business purpose," Al noted years later. "The purpose was to apply our unique distillation technology to community development. What really intrigued Spencer was the favorable economics of integrated on-site utilities that could potentially free community enterprises and community entrepreneurs from zoning, planning, and licensing hurdles presented by conventional utilities. . . . Spencer described the company as 'a libertarian venture specializing in water treatment technology and energy management oriented towards community utility systems.'"[19]

Spencer initially got involved with Terraqua as an investor and soon became friends with the engineers working there. When the company ran into financial difficulties due to unscrupulous investors who were undermining the business, the engineers, who were also stockholders, asked Spencer to step in as CEO. Al was too busy on the engineering side to do so, and that wasn't his area of expertise. Nor was it Spencer's, but he did everything he could to save the company, an attempt that ultimately failed.

"Some investors had hired a manager who deliberately tried to destroy the company," Spencer explained. "One thing he (the manager) did was remove the quality control at the end of the production line, which led to all kinds of problems with customers. Apparently, his idea was that the company would go under and be put on the auction block, then the investors could buy all the assets for next to nothing. It was a pretty disappointing situation, especially since the distillation technology was sound and worked well. It could have provided Los Angeles with ultra-pure water at a low cost."[20]

An Engineer's Engineer

"I met Alvin in about 1989 through John Fowler," recalls Bob Benz, engineer and founder of Benz Air Engineering. "Alvin helped me with many engineering projects over the years. He was an expert in both mechanical and chemical engineering. He was quite well-versed and a huge resource. He would come over to my place in Hermosa, oftentimes after doing testing on an engine we jointly developed. He would hold court with a whole group of us, surfers, bar owners, bar patrons. We would have very involved discussions that were quite jovial and often involved some high-end bourbon. He had a lot of different insights, and we would get into arguments and discussions. Some of the surfers called him Grandpa Walton because he was always sporting his overalls. He was also called 'the professor' or 'Einstein' because he really did look like Einstein. He was very smart and opinionated, but he was also quite humble.

"Man, let me tell you," Bob added, "the development of our engine was quite humbling for all of us. It's a big block

Chevy variant, V8, bore-and-stroke 454. It burns natural gas and produces electricity. Whereas most engines are cooled by water through a radiator, we cooled it with the engine water jacket, which produces steam. It's a co-generation system that's unique in that the engine can operate twenty-four hours a day with maximum torque and no throttle. It generates power for less than four cents a kilowatt hour. The engine will cost $10,000 to $15,000 and will generate revenue for a facility in the range of $300,000 to $500,000 a year. It has a very attractive place in the near future for producing power. I call it the solution to the renewable grid.

"The engine was codesigned by Alvin based on some work he'd done earlier on projects that were eventually dropped," Bob explained. "One of those had an ancillary process of making chilled water out of a modified turbocharger. The engine was driven by low-pressure steam, which created about seventy gallons a minute of forty-five-degree water. Alvin had also developed a high altitude, post-piston engine that ran on nitro methane for a NASA prototype. Then there was a cam engine where, instead of the pistons being connected to a crank shaft, they were connected to a cam shaft, so he could vary their position. That design could, theoretically, generate power with over 65 percent efficiency.

"Alvin also ran his own businesses along the way," said Bob. "One of them had a distillation system for desalinizing water. The units worked great. In fact, I still have a couple of them. We used them to distill beer into whiskey and make moonshine. Alvin had many different research projects that grew out of his inventive mind. He was just a treasure trove of information."

Lanny Trefz, owner of LTR Racing Engines, agrees with Bob's assessment. "Al was a genius, but he was also a real character. We laughed and joked a lot and had good times together. He'd sit in his chair and slap his legs and laugh so hard he couldn't breathe. He liked his Corona and a lime. He was such a unique person to know and a great guy. Early in our friendship he bought me some automotive books and taught me how to use a slide rule. When I was in my twenties, I wanted to join the Society of Automotive Engineers, but I didn't have a college degree. He wrote a letter asking them to count my experience and got me into the society. When I came up with an ignition system for race cars, he helped me get it patented. Neither of us made any money though. We just did stuff because we wanted to do it. We'd put hundreds of hours into a project but didn't charge the customers for it all. If we added up all the hours over a few years, it'd be more than a half million dollars for a project, so we'd cut it in half so as not to make them mad."

Al had a saying with regard to business: "You can cut a man's hair many times, but you can only scalp him once." He worked hard to give his customers good service time after time, but he never scalped them.

While running or contributing to businesses and consulting with other engineers, like Bob and Lanny, Al found time to research and write about technical areas of interest and design and build patentable devices. ResearchGate lists fifteen of his scientific publications, which include:

- "A New Approach to the Design of a Diesel Engine for General Aviation Aircraft Propulsion"
- "A Method for Evaluating the Atmospheric Ozone Impact of Actual Vehicle Emissions"
- "Supplementary Fueling of Four-Stroke-Cycle Automotive Diesel Engines by Propane Fumigation"
- "Fuel Economy Potential of a Combined Engine Cooling and Waste Heat Driven Automotive Air-Conditioning System"
- "Solar Thermal Absorption Heat Pump Breakeven Coefficient of Performance"
- "Compression Ignition Engine Fumigation System"
- "Hydraulic Resistance in Two-Phase Flow and Its Dependence on the Froude Number"[21]

Some of Al's research led to domestic and foreign patents. JUSTIA Patents lists a dozen of them for inventions as diverse as reciprocating engines, fuel injection systems, heat pumps, automotive air-conditioning systems, and a manufacturing method for cellulose fiber insulation.[22]

Government Bureaucracies

As a scientist, Al was interested in technologies that could have a large-scale benefit for society, like desalinization and nuclear energy. He was frustrated by government bureaucracies that stifled innovation to protect the status quo. In an article he coauthored with Chas Holloway, they traced how government took over the electrical industry shortly after its inception and consistently ignored new technologies they didn't control. Thorium reactors were a case in point:

> Not long after World War II, nuclear fission reactors were designed and built to produce heat that could be used for electricity generation. Uranium-based reactors were built, not just to produce electricity, but also weapons-grade plutonium. This work was initiated by The Atomic Energy commission (AEC), which had been formed in 1946 to replace the wartime Manhattan Project. Its stated mission was to develop peaceful uses of the atom. But in many ways, they did just the opposite.
>
> It had been suggested that other, more plentiful elements than uranium might be found to produce nuclear energy. Thorium was the only other naturally-occurring fissionable element known. Thus, since 1950, thorium fuel cycle reactors were built and successfully used to produce thermal energy. Between 1965 and 1968, such reactors operated for over 15,000 hours. This prompted AEC Chairman, Glenn Seaborg, to announce that the thorium-fueled reactor was successful. However, facing the Cold War arms race, the government decided to concentrate on the uranium system for its nuclear bomb-making capabilities, and in 1973 it officially discontinued all work on thorium.[23]

"The growth of civilization will require more and more energy," Lowi and Holloway concluded. "That's an irrefutable fact. Will entrepreneurs convince U.S. politicians—who seized power over energy production during the FDR years—to allow this technology? Or will our politicians watch other nation-states develop it first? How long will our politicians watch, afraid to act? How long will they hope the future won't happen? Thorium-cycle reactors may seem like a panacea. But, unfortunately, there's one thing they cannot do: stop government bureaucracy."[24]

Al's frustration was exacerbated by personal experience with government bureaucracies standing in the way of his innovations that could improve society. Bruce Canter gives two examples: "Al tried to get involved with the Santa Barbara desalination project but was turned down because his patented process used a heat engine that raised environmental concerns. Al asked them, 'Where do you get your electricity to run your pumps for your reverse osmosis process?' It turned out it was a coal plant in Arizona. It wasn't really about limiting pollution; it was about importing the power from far away at a cost and creating pollution there. Al explained to me this was just a form of NIMBYism (Not In My Back Yard). Al's system should have been a hit with environmentalists since it used absorption distillation that mimicked the natural conversion of seawater into rain. It's a slower process, but it's more natural. Al's approach wasn't trying to control nature or disregard it, but to be more harmonious with it.

"Then there was the incident with Los Angeles Metro Bus," Bruce continued. "Al had a patent on a dual-fuel engine that ran on diesel and gasoline. There was a trade-off in the emissions with a dramatic decrease in particulates and a slight increase in nitric oxide. Metro wanted to do it because the engine also had lower combustion temperatures, which meant they would last longer. But ultimately, the AQMD (Air Quality Management District) wouldn't buy in because they didn't like the trade-off. In both Santa Barbara and LA, the bureaucracies didn't bother with a cost-benefit analysis that made sense. Because Al's designs would increase something negative, they couldn't see the larger benefit."

Al also believed a cost-benefit analysis should be applied to nuclear energy, of which he was a staunch supporter. "Al and I had many conversations over the years about this," Bruce said. "It's ironic that environmentalists today are speaking more favorably of the latest nuclear technology because there's no carbon footprint. Al was skeptical about human-caused climate change, but he would say to such environmentalists: 'If that's your concern, here's the solution.' He was really good at this kind of cost-benefit analysis that most people shy away from because they want absolutes. It went with his overarching philosophy that you just do the best you can and try to do even better the next time. There are no certainties, no absolutes. It's all about doing your best with what you have."

Al used to quote a mock Latin aphorism in regard to short sighted people: *Illegitimi non carborundum.* It has no literal meaning but is translated as "Don't let the bastards grind you down."[25]

He didn't.

▼

Looking back on Al's long and varied career, daughter Rosie pointed out, "Dad's ideas were honed in practice as a businessman, an entrepreneur, and an inventor. If you read his writings in chronological order, you can see how his thinking evolved to where he became even more philosophical and theoretical about coming to grips with politics. He had a lot of disdain for it."

While Al's thinking about politics and government was shaped by his business experiences, a larger influence were the people he met while working in the aerospace industry, especially Andrew Galambos. Their relationship is the subject of the next chapter.

LIBERTY WITHOUT INDIVIDUALISM IS UNTHINKABLE
INDIVIDUALISM WITHOUT CAPITALISM IS IMPOSSIBLE

FREE ENTERPRISE INSTITUTE

5641 EAST BEVERLY BLVD.
LOS ANGELES, CALIF. 90022
PHONES 264-1776 ● 721-1776
(AREA CODE 213)

ALVIN LOWI, JR.
SENIOR LECTURER
RES. PHONE 832-5622

Alvin Jr's calling card of the Free Enterprise Institute, circa mid-1960s

CHAPTER

A Lasting Encounter

*My social "enlightenment" (such as it is) began with
my friendship with Joseph A. Galambos. . . . My skepticism
regarding some aspects of Galambos's approach will not obscure
my genuine admiration of the man and his work.*
—Alvin Lowi Jr

A ndrew Joseph Galambos (1924–1997) was born in Hungary and came to New York as a child. His father was an architect and liberal thinker who foresaw a Second World War on the horizon and wanted to get his family out of harm's way. His plan didn't quite work. When war did come, Andrew volunteered for the U.S. Army. Afterward, he got his undergrad degree at City College of New York and a master's degree at the University of Minnesota, where he met and married Suzanne Siegel in 1949. He earned all the credits for a PhD in physics but never did a dissertation, perhaps because of his lifelong reluctance to write.

Three years later the Galamboses moved to Los Angeles and Andrew went to work for North American Aviation, and then Space Technology Laboratory (STL), a division of Ramo-Wooldridge Corporation. Al Lowi joined Ramo-Wooldridge in 1957, and the two would have a long and fruitful relationship. Here's how Al remembered their early days:

> Andrew J. Galambos (aka Joseph A. Galambos) was a colleague of the author's when both were members of the technical staff of Ramo-Wooldridge, later to become TRW Space Technology Laboratories. This was during the formative period of the aerospace industry when most engineers did not know the difference between an airplane and an artificial earth satellite. There, Galambos, a highly regarded astrophysicist, presented a popular noontime lecture series to other technical staff members which he called "Astronomy, Astrophysics and Astronautics" (1957–59). Subsequently, he offered similar lecture courses to his students and to the public during a brief tenure as a professor of physics, mathematics and astronomy at Whittier College. This led to his founding The Free Enterprise Institute in Monterey Park, CA, in 1960, through which he developed and presented similar courses subject to tuition including his memorable "Course 100," entitled "Capitalism: The Key to Survival." The author was first a student and then a lecturer, having taught this course during 1962–64 under the strict supervision of Galambos. As a result, the author developed both an appreciation for and a divergence from Galambos's ideas, which readers familiar with this background will surely recognize.[26]

Social Enlightenment

After Galambos's death, Al wrote more in depth about their mutually beneficial association in the article "A Lasting Encounter." The next section is an abridged version of that piece because, who better to tell the story of their collaborations, and confrontations, than one of the participants?

Galambos and I were colleagues on the technical staff of the Air Force consultancy Ramo-Wooldridge before that company became TRW. On the side, Galambos was an entrepreneur and proud of it. Right away I could see he was eccentric. Here was this highly credentialed physicist who owned a securities and insurance dealership. Galambos was in partnership with another colleague, Donald H. Allen. (Don was a mathematician.) On close examination, they were not only selling securities on company time but also CAPITALISM, for Gawd's sakes.

At the time, I was a struggling graduate student in engineering at UCLA, and Galambos generously tutored me in thermodynamics, kinetic theory, and scientific method, among other things. He also sold me an income-protection insurance policy and some mutual fund shares for which he got a commission. His forthright and expert explanation of this transaction captured my interest in his free-enterprise ideas.

Don Allen subscribed to *The Freeman*, which he read religiously. He got Galambos interested in this material on the basis of improving his exposition of laissez faire capitalism. . . . My preparations for language readings and qualifying exams put me behind Galambos and Allen in apprehending the new social enlightenment flowing from the pages of *The Freeman*. Soon enough, however, we all came to realize our employment made us part and parcel of a racket that, in principle, was not unlike the one against which we were supposed to be defending America. Subsequently, Galambos shucked the aerospace boondoggle and joined the faculty of Whittier College to teach physics, math, and astronomy. He still had his Universal Shares and continued his ideological campaign with the students. When he decided to offer his lectures on capitalism during the weekly chapel period in competition with the college chaplain, his tenure was terminated.

In the fall of 1960, Galambos went home to New York City to meet the folks at the Foundation for Economic Education (FEE) and at the Nathaniel Branden Institute, Ayn Rand's front at the time. Ostensibly, he was out to research and implement a kindred venture in Southern California. I tagged along as though we were taking the "Yellow Brick Road" to Gotham to find the "wizards" of freedom.

So it was through Galambos and after Allen that I was introduced to the wonderful world of Read, Mises, Hazlitt, Rothbard, Harper, LeFevre, Chodorov, Bastiat, Weaver, etc. And I must say it was most reassuring to find that Galambos was not alone in believing that laissez faire capitalism was THE way of human life in the world as it is. But then came the realization that building ballistic missiles had nothing to do with building civilization, which created something of a dilemma for those of us who, unlike Galambos, had no entrepreneurial experience.

Curiously, each of us (Galambos, Allen, and I) had previously and independently bonded with Rand, Paine, and Thoreau. So by the time we met, we were already confirmed individualists and Americanists. But until our exposure to the "Austrians," we were lacking key pieces of social knowledge and technology, specifically economics and free enterprise. The Austrian connection was a significant turning point for Galambos and, subsequently, for me.

Galambos readily embraced Mises's social arguments and economic conclusions, but as a physical scientist, he could not accept the Austrian notion of a priori social knowledge, any more than he could accept such hermeneutic authority in physics. He believed an authentic social science was not only possible but necessary for the future of the race. Mere authoritative opinion would not suffice. For starters, he insisted human action was as much a part of nature as planetary motion; that human nature had to be a part of the whole of the natural world, and that bona fide economic knowledge would have to hold up to the proceedings of natural science.

With postulates and definitions appropriate to the social domain of phenomena, Galambos expected the subject to yield to the scientific method in its entirety as does all natural history. He explained how an a priori deductive exercise consisting of reasoning alone, which comprises only the middle part of the scientific method, would fail to accredit economic knowledge to the degree necessary to overcome controversy. He showed how a complete round of scientific endeavor must include an a posteriori inductive struggle at the beginning and an observational test of the deductive projections at the end to escape the appearance of dogma. He would have agreed with the declaration of Hayek's friend Karl Popper, "If it can't be falsified, it isn't science, economic or other." Predictably, Mises was offended by these notions, but then, after all was said and done, Galambos was not an "economist" and he paid good money and delivered enthusiastic audiences.

Suzanne Galambos (Andrew's long-suffering wife), Don Allen, and I comprised the original staff of Galambos's Free Enterprise Institute. Initially, Galambos was the sole faculty member in residence. All the courses were his, starting with a 20-lecture offering called "Course 100: Capitalism: The Key to Survival" in the spring of 1961. Galambos was eager to have scholars he admired visit and speak to his students. The first such invited lecturer was Professor Ludwig von Mises, whose 1962 seminar in Los Angeles that Galambos promoted was attended by me and many other seekers asking similar questions as Galambos. Shortly after Mises's visit, Galambos arranged seminars for Leonard Read and F. A. Harper. These meetings were well attended and it was all very stimulating and inspiring.

Looking back, I don't know how I could have lived without the experience. Galambos also scheduled and promoted a seminar for Spencer Heath, but that one had to be cancelled because of Heath's age and failing health. He longed to host Ayn Rand in "his" market but she spurned him. She would have none of Galambos as long as she had Branden. (Branden was much better looking.)

Like Galambos, I never answered to the nom de guerre "libertarian." It was always easier for me to identify with the apolitical and historical sense of the term "liberalism" as embodied in Galambos's ideological challenge. When Galambos debated Leonard Read on the need for a new public label for the laissez-faire paradigm, I sided with Galambos. Galambos like Mises, Hayek, and other Europeans of the laissez-faire persuasion considered themselves "liberals" in keeping with that respectable tradition. The world could go to hell before they would relinquish this word to a bunch of erstwhile American fascists. Galambos even used "The Liberal" as a pseudonym and named his parent company in the ideology business "The Liberal Institute of Natural Science and Technology," abbreviated "LIONS Tech."

When I need a label, "liberal" suits me fine. I realize it takes more than a sport coat to make a sport, and I enjoy an argument on the level of "who owns it," a rhetorical device Galambos made potent. Galambos considered the liberal label a weapon in a war of ideas. He saw any opportunity to challenge the legitimacy of FDR's political heirs, the New

Deal thugs and their descendants, as a valuable one. He considered the usurpation of this label by fascists to be pernicious and insisted such use should be challenged at every opportunity. I notice some libertarians refer to themselves on occasion as classical liberals. They could well admire how Galambos was able to make that rhetorical device a shining badge of distinction.

Galambos has been characterized as "one of the oddest characters in the shadows of libertarian history." There is no denying he was an oddity, but perhaps no more so than Mises in terms of an uncompromising posture in the teaching of well-considered principles. But unlike the academic Mises, who suffered at the discretion of tenured academics and bureaucratic university administrators, Galambos was an entrepreneur who anguished over the usurpations of the regulatory bureaucrats and tax collectors. As an uncompromising preacher as well as a practitioner of profit-seeking proprietorship, he was in a class by himself. As he might well have expounded in a five-hour lecture with no breaks, I will venture to boil down his thesis to three simple and familiar prescriptions: (1) do no harm, (2) live and let live, and (3) to each his own. His overarching principle that profit is virtuous would take longer to explain.

That Galambos is possibly "in the shadows of libertarian history" is a consequence of his radical ideas on intellectual property. His so-called theory of primary property had the effect of discouraging publication or extrapolation of any aspects of his teachings by any of his students while, at the same time, he himself suffered a writers' paralysis. (See my essay "On Andrew Galambos and His Primary Property Ideas."[27]) Nevertheless, Galambos's influence has been penetrating, unmistakable, undeniable, and creative. During the period 1957 to about 1982, he persuaded thousands of adults to pay him to convince them he was right.

What set Galambos apart from others in the "freedom" movement was his utter disdain for politics and non-profit organization. He was completely liberated from the polls and he celebrated the individual human profit motive as the engine of creation. He described a "not-for-profit" declaration and application to the state for a tax exemption as a blatantly hypocritical gesture of voluntary servitude and poverty. Such eleemosynary status he considered not only unnatural and anti-capitalistic but also a seeking after legal privilege by tax-hustling panderers to the state. He upheld proprietary administration as the total alternative to politics and bureaucracy, describing all manner of innovative possibilities for the delivery of public services by voluntary market means. For him, private property was the only rational and moral basis for authority in society and he was out to buttress this audacious hypothesis with scientific verification, a quest he called "Volitional Science."[28]

Shunned Collaborator

The previous section was Al's take on Galambos. Others have shared their perspective on the man, including onetime presidential candidate Harry Browne, who wrote:

He was a fascinating mixture of contrasts. He combined a brilliant mind with an ungracious personality. He was an astrophysicist who taught social science. He preached the importance of respect for intellectual property, but freely lifted the ideas of others without giving them credit. He was dishonest, but he inspired others to be more honest. He disdained the word "libertarian" while turning thousands of people into libertarians. He was an insensitive teacher, and yet he apparently changed the lives of most of the people he taught. And he pushed out of his own life practically everyone who was important to him. One of those people was Alvin Lowi—a long-time friend and business associate of Galambos, who had taught some of his courses.[29]

A falling-out between the two men seemed inevitable, as Galambos seemed incapable of lasting friendships. There appear to be several reasons for the eventual split. Jeff Solomon, Al's friend and Galambos's student, remembers Al telling him that he was fired from the institute because he wanted to be fired. "He got into some arguments with Galambos because he knew where that would lead,' Jeff recalls. "And sure enough, Galambos asked him to leave. That freed Al philosophically in very fundamental ways. His was a deep-rooted departure from Galambos's approach. Although a lot of their conclusions were similar, there were some deep divides between them. When Al left the institute, Galambos asked him to sign something that he would agree not to compete with him. And Al kind of just worked his thing instead of having an institute. Galambos loved to talk but he never got around to writing, whereas Al put more energy into writing."

"Al also told me he wanted to be fired," Chas Holloway confirmed. "It was because Al didn't believe that volitional science was ready for prime time yet. Galambos wanted to put something out there. He was satisfied with it the way it was, assuming he could fix it later. Al insisted on more research. That was the issue that broke them up. Al wanted to continue doing research on the principles that Galambos was talking about whereas Galambos wanted to say, 'Okay, that's done. Let's market it.'

"Galambos and Lowi were tight," Holloway added. "They were buddies and did everything together. But Al told me after the breakup he only talked to Galambos once for the rest of their lives. I think that was mostly on Galambos's part."

Al did not touch on some of the pricklier parts of his relationship with Galambos in print, but others who knew and appreciated both men, did. Fred G. Marks and Allison J. Marks gave a few other reasons for the separation: "Working with Galambos, Lowi listened to a recording of each Galambos lecture of Course 100 and the following week Lowi would replicate that lecture in his own presentation of Course 100. . . . Galambos was unhappy with Lowi[']s practice of holding lengthy after-class discussions with Lowi[']s Course 100 students, and Lowi was unhappy with Galambos's restriction on such discussions. . . . In consequence of Lowi's dissatisfaction, in 1963, he proposed to Galambos that Jay Snelson take his place as an FEI lecturer."[30]

Another issue the Marks mentioned was a proposed Galambos book: "By 1963–1964 Galambos had been talking to his colleagues and students about writing a book presenting the ideas of Course 100 and Course F-201. Since Galambos was very busy with his lectures, in or about 1964 Alvin Lowi proposed to write a book setting forth Galambos's ideas and to print a limited edition of one hundred serial-numbered copies of that book, all within one year. Lowi had obtained commitments for a total of $50,000 for production of such a book from around twenty to twenty-five individuals who were interested in seeing Galambos's ideas perpetuated in book form. The purchasing power of $50,000 in 1964 was equivalent to a purchasing power of $375,000 in 2013.

Galambos turned down this offer.[31] He said the subscription price was outrageously high and he would not sanction any book of his to be so "overpriced."[32] (Galambos died in 1997, and two years later some of his taped FEI lectures were published in a book called *Sic Itur Ad Astra*.) But according to Holloway, "the idea that Galambos would not sanction any book of his being so overpriced was just an excuse. Al told me he believed that Galambos took writing a book very seriously and was afraid of some secret flaw in his theory coming to light, specifically a circularity in his definition of property."

Galambos's treatment of friends like Al was the rule, not the exception. Harry Browne observes, "According to Alvin Lowi, in Galambos' early days in Los Angeles he was gracious, thoughtful, and hospitable. But after his courses made him important to people, he apparently no longer felt the need to be gracious. By the time I met him in late 1963, his personality had changed." Browne went on to say one of those changes was to become parsimonious with giving credit where due: "And on some of the rare occasions when he gave specific credit to a living person, it was backhanded. When he did, it was usually only in general terms rather than for any identifiable contributions to his philosophy. For example, Alvin Lowi was Andrew's closest associate and a great intellectual stimulus to him. But in all of Andrew's lectures I attended, I heard him give credit to Alvin only once."[33]

According to Chuck Estes, an FEI alumnus, Al played a key role not only in the evolution of Galambos's ideas but in assembling the cohort who would pass them along: "Some of Galambos' early students and supporters included Harry Browne, . . . George Haddad, . . . Richard Nesbit, . . . Billy Robbins, . . . Jerome Smith, . . . With the exception of Billy Robbins, Alvin Lowi was chiefly responsible for recruiting this distinguished early cadre. It was he who originally persuaded Joe, then a fellow employee at TRW, to found the Free Enterprise Institute and teach his ideas."[34]

Jay Snelson, whom Al proposed as his successor, was senior lecturer and professor of volitational science at FEI from 1964 to 1978. He also saw Al as critical to the creation and success of the institute: "It seems to me unlikely that Galambos would have ever founded his Institute without his accidental encounter with you [Al] and Don."[35]

Sara Taft, Al's close friend of sixty years, recalled how she met him in 1962 at a Galambos course he was teaching. "We talked several times afterward, and he explained a lot of things that made sense to me. I was very interested in esoteric things and the metaphysical world, as I was into astrology. He was quite astute in physics and science and would connect the metaphysical world to the physical world.

"He was an artist when it came to communication and also a brilliant teacher," she added. "Nothing stumped him. I was always amazed at how he handled people who disagreed with him with such grace. He would explain things in a way that didn't make them feel like they were in opposition. He would extend the frame in which the question was being asked so they could both see what was being talked about. Galambos couldn't do that. If you disagreed with Galambos, he barked at you. Al didn't bark. He offered you honey."

ᗺ

Al never pushed for credit for his seminal influence on Galambos's ideas or institute, although their contemporaries were quick to do so. He also never hesitated to mention his indebtedness to Galambos or to promote Galambos's revolutionary insights to others. He wrote:

> Galambos was one of few thinkers who conceived of private, profit-seeking businesses providing comprehensive property protection services as the keystone of human society. His reliance on competitive private enterprise to deliver protective services—for a profit—is a monumental idea. While the practice is yet to come to fruition on a large scale, we now know that it is the only

reliable method of obtaining property protection consistent with liberty. Since Galambos is no longer with us, it is up to us to pass along his ideas and manner of thinking to the next generation.[36]

Alvin Jr. and Spencer H. MacCallum, San Pedro, California
circa mid to late 1970s

CHAPTER 6

The Two Spencers

In writing this foreword to Spencer Heath MacCallum's biography,
I struggled to stay on the subject. I was drawn instead to
reflecting on my own indebtedness to the person who had
the greatest influence on my intellectual life, as well as
having been my closest friend of more than 60 years.
—Alvin Lowi Jr.

In the last chapter we looked at the impact Andrew Galambos had on Al's life, and vice versa. Here we'll consider two other men Al met during his association with Galambos who had perhaps an even larger impact: Spencer Heath (1876–1963), and his grandson and namesake, Spencer Heath MacCallum (1931–2020).

"During my association with Galambos," Al once wrote, "I became acquainted with engineer-inventor-attorney-industrialist Spencer Heath and his grandson, anthropologist Spencer Heath MacCallum. Heath was one of the founders of the Henry George School and had recently published a treatise entitled *Citadel, Market and Altar: Emerging Society*. Heath was up in age and in frail health by then but I found his grandson MacCallum to be a worthy heir to his work on society."[37]

Spencer Heath

Al's comments about Heath are from his various tributes and articles about him.[38] In a summary of his background, Al noted, "After earlier successful careers as a professional engineer and a practicing patent attorney, Spencer Heath became widely known as a pioneer in early aviation. In 1907, with his law client Emile Berliner, he successfully demonstrated the helicopter principle—that rotary blades can lift the weight of an engine from the earth. Later he developed the first machine mass production of airplane propellers and supplied most of the propellers used by the Allies in the First World War. In the summer of 1929, Heath sold all of his patents and technical facilities and two years later retired from business to devote himself fully to the study of his longtime interest, the philosophy of science.

"It was very late in his life when I [Al] met Spencer Heath. My first impression was that of a dignified and cultivated southern gentleman, a reserved but at the same time intensely self-assured man who was deeply absorbed in thought regarding some new ideas. At the time, 1961, I was traveling in some strident libertarian company that was driven to doing something about mankind's ominous collectivist predicament. Mr. Heath appeared curiously tranquil vis-a-vis our burning concerns. At the same time, he was ambitious out of all proportion to his age to put forth a message concerning what he called, simply, 'physics.' He was especially eager to reach professionally qualified and academically recognized physicists in the hope that they would want to carry what he considered the real merit of his life's work into the mainstream of physics.

"Mr. Heath's speech was little more than a whisper and he had an aversion for using forceful or authoritative expressions or gestures. A frail physique indicated his advancing years. (He celebrated his 86th birthday with my family at our home in Torrance, California on January 3, 1962.) These difficulties notwithstanding, accepting them as trifling deceptions of appearance, he was constantly making his opportunity for disclosure, even among presumptuous, impatient and loquacious conversationalists such as myself.

"A major objective of Heath's was to help birth an authentic natural science of society, meaning a science that could generate dependable social technology. Discovering what the existing successful sciences had in common, he published in *Citadel, Market and Altar* an initial outline of a wholly rational science of society, successfully bridging for the first time the gap between the quantitative and the qualitative. He believed that in science, as in any other field, the psychological prerequisite for discovery is aesthetic motivation under the inspiration of beauty—pursuing for its own sake beauty dimly seen or intuited. He also believed that the most profound gift we can offer our fellow human beings, our most valued service, is inspiration."

Spencer MacCallum

Spencer Heath MacCallum was born in New York City in 1931. His maternal grandfather, Spencer Heath, aka Popdaddy, took a particular interest in him from birth. Young Spencer and Popdaddy had a close relationship, but it wasn't until Spencer went to Princeton that he started to understand Popdaddy's ideas about philosophy and politics. He never was quite able to comprehend Popdaddy's physics. After graduation, Spencer went to the University of Washington and got his master's in social anthropology. During his college years, Popdaddy introduced him to leading philosophical thinkers like E. C. Riegel, Murray Rothbard, Charley Reese, Russell Kirk, and F. A. "Baldy" Harper. The latter became Spencer's mentor. Then there was the California connection, which is how Spencer wound up in the home of Frances Norton Manning in Santa Ana, where he met Andrew Galambos and Alvin Lowi Jr.

Unlike his relationship with Spencer Heath, whom Al only got to know for two brief years before his death, Al's relationship with Spencer McCallum lasted more than six decades. After MacCallum's death, Al penned the foreword to his biography, in which he called Spencer "my closest friend of more than 60 years." Al went on to write:

> My relationship with Spencer was somewhat broader than merely witnessing his achievements. Besides a long, warm, and unwavering friendship and family embrace, I had the benefit of Spencer's insight and encouragement in my work to explain the scientific method and apply it to the development of an authentic natural science of society. Spencer believed my preparation and experience in the physical sciences, a preparation he lacked and for which he felt handicapped, would be

instrumental in this crucial development. He was keen to have me develop his grandfather's unpublished ideas on the philosophy and epistemology of natural science, accounting for modern relativity and quantum considerations.

Spencer's life was a pageant to behold. It was one unheralded adventure after another of his own making. He led a charmed life and was beloved by many. His enthusiasm for every opportunity to venture was so contagious, yet his remarkable and varied experience was not apparent to those he encountered casually because of his unassuming modesty.[39]

The respect was mutual. For his part, Spencer said of Al:

He helped stretch my intellectual grasp well beyond where it was with Popdaddy and F. A. Baldy. In particular, I gained an appreciation of the meaning and implications of the scientific method. He became well acquainted with Popdaddy in the time before Popdaddy died. Popdaddy and Al talked about engineering, aviation, and physics. Al gradually picked up on Popdaddy's consuming interest in the philosophy of science. Using the scientific method as a way to understand society was one of Popdaddy's important ideas. As an engineer, he was very interested in how to apply the scientific method, with its emphasis on experiment, to social organization. It was unfortunate that Popdaddy became ill and had to return home just when they were building such key relationships.[40]

"Dad's relationship with Spencer transcended that of many of his other friends," says Al's son, Alvin III. "Dad had some extremely loyal and very good friends, but his relationship with Spencer was special."

"I remember meeting Spencer MacCallum as a child," Rosie fondly recalls. "We called him Uncle Penny. He used to come to our house and take care of us when my parents would go away. He was a mentor for me in high school. I almost went into anthropology because of him. There was always an excitement and energy surrounding Spencer and everything he did. He was kind of eccentric, but he actually lived out his ideas."

"Al was absolutely passionate about his friendships with people like Spencer, who shared his philosophies," his sister Bettie remembers. "He was extremely proud of Spencer. You can see it in the foreword he wrote for Spencer's biography; it's a beautiful piece of writing. You can feel the passion he had for the work they did together."

Al and Spencer collaborated on papers and worked on cataloging Heath's extensive and mostly unpublished intellectual estate through the Heather Foundation.[41] Spencer set up the foundation for "furthering understanding of society as an evolving natural phenomenon of spontaneously patterned cooperation among freely-acting individuals."[42] The foundation administered the literary estate trusts of Spencer Heath, Arthur C. Holden, and E. C. Riegel.

Al and Spencer's partnerships weren't just intellectual. Spencer invested in, and later joined, Al's business, Terraqua, an ambitious water desalination project near Los Angeles (see chapter 4 for more details). The business ran afoul of utility regulations and unscrupulous investors and went under, but its demise didn't affect Al and Spencer's friendship, even though it cost Spencer his sizable investment.

Masterworks

If Heath's magnum opus was *Citadel, Market and Altar* (1957), MacCallum's was *The Art of Community* (1970), a title suggested by Al. Both books had a profound influence on Al and countless others. Chris Boehr, a student of Galambos and a friend of Lowi and MacCallum, notes why: "Spencer Heath had an enormous influence on Al because he showed a way you can make a society without a state and still provide all the public goods, like national defense, police, courts, legal systems, the whole thing, which was explained in his book *Citadel, Market and Altar*."

For Al, this book provided a better outline for society than other systems, like socialism or libertarianism. He explored and expanded Heath's model in his monograph "Constructing a Science of Society: A Trial Based on the Universal Integrity of Property Principle." Here's Al's abridged summary of Heath's main ideas:

Where individuals, through cooperation, evolve forms of spontaneous order, we see the development of society. In Heath's concept, population alone is not sufficient to constitute society; behavior is the key. Wherever in a population we observe individuals freely engaging in reciprocal relations, there and to that extent only, are we observing society. With the maturation of society, we have the emergence of a distinctly new life form on the earth, a biological organism marked by a function not shared by any other, namely, the potential to interact creatively with its environment so as not to exhaust and despoil it but to make it progressively more capable of supporting its own kind of life—and not necessarily at the expense of any other.

Examining this emerging life form, Heath recognized three functional aspects, symbolically expressed in the title of his major work as *Citadel, Market and Altar*. The first was the defensive, or protective, function, affording that security of persons and property upon which all else rests. This he might have called the integrity function, since it has to do with maintaining the integrity of the constituent units—individuals. While this can require the use of defensive force, the major part of this function is provided by voluntary or customary observance of the distinctly social institution of property.

The second function, symbolized as Market, was that of exchange, whereby men attend to one another's biological needs with benefit to each and sacrifice of none. It maintains the organism alive at any given level but is not, in and of itself, progressive.

If Citadel and Market denote the immune function and the metabolic function, respectively, then Altar symbolizes the psyche, for it includes all of those non-necessitous activities men engage in for their own sake alone, the aesthetic and recreational arts, religion, philosophy, pure research in the sciences, and the like. If the Market maintains the society alive at a given level, the Altar through its discoveries feeding back new technologies into the marketplace advances society to new levels, ever enabling it to transcend itself.

As the Citadel enables the Market with greater and greater efficiency to solve the problems of sustaining life, so the Market, by progressively freeing men and women from bondage to biological need and natural risk, grants them passage into the realm of the Altar— the realm of creative artistry, inspiration, and motivation to higher goals.

In *Citadel, Market and Altar*, published in 1957 and now out of print, Heath outlined his rationale for a natural science of society and explored in some detail one proposed application of social technology, a means whereby he thought the marketplace, under normal profit motivation, could and ultimately would undertake to provide all public services, replacing the present tax-based and insolvent administration of our public communities. For the name of the new natural science of society, he suggested a little used but already existing word, socionomy, defined by *Webster's New International Dictionary* as, "the theory or formulation of the organic laws exemplified in the organization and development of society."[43]

Spencer MacCallum would expand on his grandfather's ideas about society in his groundbreaking book *The Art of Community*, of which one reviewer wrote:

> MacCallum has opened the door to some interesting speculation. Imagine an aggregation of proprietary communities making up an urban complex. Suppose every city in the nation gradually evolved to this pattern? Why not the entire planet? If one is governed by contractual obligations, the sum of which is the constitution of the community in which one happens to be at a given time, then what is the function of even a limited political government?
>
> This is without question one of the most thought-provoking books ever published on the subject of alternatives to government as we know it. *The Art of Community* invites us to look to the area of alternatives to political, tax supported institutions, one of the least surveyed and most promising intellectual and entrepreneurial frontiers of the modern world.[44]

Heath and MacCallum suggested an alternative to politically corrupt government in the form of proprietary communities that could provide public services. "It was a breakthrough," Al insisted, "because it is precisely that aspect of human life—the quest for community—that provides the traditional excuse for politics and taxation, which inevitably lead away from community toward human bondage."[45]

But isn't all this speculating and theorizing about a society free from politics and government a waste of time since we will never achieve such a society? Al and Spencer didn't think so. They believed it was better to head in the right direction even if you never quite reached your final destination. They shared the idealism of Spencer's early mentor, F. A. "Baldy" Harper. "He had a great sense of optimism about the future," Spencer said. "He adopted the concept of a 'total alternative' to political government—a phrase of mine that he and several others adopted. This became his ideal goal by which to correct and guide mundane decisions much as the North Star enables the mariner to make continuous course corrections. The mariner doesn't expect to reach the star, but steering by it—a process of small decisions and course corrections—he eventually reaches his destination. Baldy believed we needed a transcendent ideal to guide our everyday decisions and keep us on the path heading toward freedom."

Al acknowledged his debt to Spencer in "The Legacy of Spencer Heath":

As a life-long devotee of the scientific method and an advocate of its universal applicability in all areas of human experience, I should have come around more quickly to appreciate the revolutionary and cosmic nature of Heath's inquiries and to see the merit of his achievements, as much for his method as for his particular discoveries, insights, and deductions. Most significant perhaps, for me, his work demonstrated how scientific philosophy forged in the discipline of mature sciences such as physics can be instructive in developing an understanding of the seemingly more complex field of social phenomena.[46]

∨

The tribute Al paid to Galambos in his monograph "Scientific Method" also applies to how he felt about Heath and MacCallum:

> I also wish I could claim more originality in this discourse. However, much of its content and many of my consequent observations were initially suggested to me by Andrew Joseph Galambos. Galambos, an astrophysicist, identified strongly with Isaac Newton. He adopted Newton's motto, "If I have seen farther than others it is because I have stood on the shoulders of giants." Similarly, while the sole responsibility for this particular elaboration is mine, I am standing on Galambos's [Heath's, and MacCallum's] shoulders.[47]

Alvin Jr. and John Imig at a Freedom of Society Meeting at John Goode's house, 2015

CHAPTER

Science of Society

I have been an observer of people (including myself)
awakening to the concept of society as a natural phenomenon
and discovering the value of scientific inquiry applied to it.
—Alvin Lowi Jr.

A l had a lifetime obsession with science and the scientific method. One of his several collaborations along these lines was the Science of Society Fellowship. "The Fellowship," he wrote, "is devoted to the application of the method of the natural sciences to social phenomena epistemologically qualified beforehand to become knowledge. The goal of such study was human progress."[48] In an overview of the fellowship, Al defined science and outlined the scientific method:

Science, the word, is etymologically derived from *Scientia*, the Latin word for "knowledge." The word "science" has come to be understood in more recent times as the method humans employ for obtaining knowledge of the natural world. The method, now known as the method of the natural sciences, has gained a consensus among thoughtful wayfarers as the only way to obtain such knowledge with sufficient confidence for the species to have survived to the present. It was defined in the works of Francis Bacon, first published in 1620 as *Novum Organum Scientiarum*—"New Instrument of Science." A careful reading of this work can discern the following four steps carried out in the order listed and repeated until a level of confidence is established in the truth of the hypothesis that motivated the inquiry in the first place. Otherwise, the hypothesis or hypotheses are unambiguously falsified. These steps of procedure are as follows:

Step 1. Ponder observations of experience with certain identifiable natural phenomena.

Step 2. Form a guess (hypothesis) as to the cause of such phenomenal events in general.

Step 3. Analyze the possible consequences of the hypothesis(-es) and develop a description of an observable event that would test the truthfulness of the hypothesis.

Step 4. Gather observational evidence that the cause hypothesized is or isn't true, i.e. faithful to reality. Valid evidence can be taken from historical events well documented as long as it meets epistemological tests for relevancy, or it can be obtained from experience contrived for the purpose under the same proviso.[49]

Al's interest in a science of society was piqued in the 1960s when he met Andrew Galambos and got involved with the Free Enterprise Institute (FEI) (see chapter 5). It was nurtured by his association with men like Spencer Heath and Spencer McCallum (see chapter 6). Heath had used the term "Science of Society" in his treatise *Citadel, Market and Altar: Emerging Society*, and had started the Science of Society Foundation in 1957.

Al worked backward and forward from this starting point. He explored society's roots as far back as Aristotle and advocated for Francis Bacon's scientific method as the key to acquiring and applying true knowledge of the human condition. He presented his developing hypotheses and theories in countless discussions and numerous writings, from short articles to book-length monographs. In 2018, toward the end of his life, he published "Constructing a Science of Society: A Trial Based on the Universal Integrity of Property Principle,"[50] an excerpt from which can be found in part two of this book. Here's an overview of his thinking from that paper:

Society is the natural phenomenon that arises in a population of autonomous human beings in communication with each other, willfully interacting and exchanging titles to objects of value to themselves without any compulsion to do so other than the natural inclinations to survive, advance and prosper. Such society is devoid of necessity for any individual participant to compromise his innate integrity as a human individual or to endure other forms of externally-imposed compulsion.

Society is characterized by economic behavior, which is the activity concerned with the utilization of scarce resources including human energy with the least effort to the maximum benefit. Economic knowledge is concerned with the minimization of resources and effort to achieve a social objective, giving rise to conservation, specializations of labor, volitional exchange, capital accumulation, innovation, employment, and entrepreneurial venturing. It has been observed that under these economic circumstances, the participants follow certain rules of order that develop spontaneously to regularize the interactions of the participants. Thereby, the society becomes self-governing, developing and delivering whatever institutional arrangements and services under entrepreneurial impetus that may be technologically sound and in economic demand.[51]

Why was Al interested in applying the scientific method to the social sciences: anthropology, sociology, psychology, economics, and political science? Why go through the trouble of imposing a "hard" scientific template on the "soft" sciences? Harkening back to Galambos, Al wrote:

Galambos himself believed the advancement of an authentic social science and a dependable social technology based on it was essential for accelerating progress toward a more autonomous and voluntary (free) society. He knew that science is the only known antidote for dogma, fantasy, and superstition, vices that impair the evolution of such a society. Indeed, science is the only check there is on arbitrary opinion, which rules human life today by default. Politics is the name of that default system.[52]

A default system, Al believed, that was thwarting human progress.

Disease and Cure

Al's personal approach to politics was to ignore it as much as possible, as Paul Mullen notes, "Al's attitude toward politics was one of 'studious abstention,' as he put it. He believed the best one could do to educate others in matters of liberty was to live his or her life as a good example. Still, he wrote his fair share of letters to the editors of local newspapers, and even to the occasional politician."

He also wrote a great deal about politics and what he saw as its toxic impact on society. "I am a naturalist when it comes to humanity and society," Al wrote in "No Conceivable Reform." "Thus, I regard politics as an epidemic disease. As I see it, 'public' health can be improved only as individual competence, initiative and prudence are perfected, practiced and spread throughout the population. These traits are not only essential for making a life worthwhile but they also provide resistance to political infection."[53]

The antidote for the infection, according to Lowi and other philosophical thinkers like Heath, MacCallum, and Galambos, was a return to the natural order of society, which could be studied like anything else in the natural world by using the scientific method. The French had a phrase for the natural order in human affairs: *laissez faire,* from the saying, *"Laissez faire et laissez passer, le monde va de lui même!"* The translation: "Let do and let pass; the world goes on by itself."[54] For the English version, one online dictionary defines *laissez faire* as "the practice or doctrine of noninterference in the affairs of others, especially with reference to individual conduct or freedom of action."[55]

Al was critical of systems that held people down and limited their opportunities. He was big on leaving people alone to make their natural way in the world. If freed from political constraint and left to themselves, Al believed humans would prosper, individually and collectively:

Human individuals acting entirely on their own recognizance under entirely natural conditions are seen to be volitional and profit-seeking. Some would say selfish to the point of greed, but that judgment says more about the critic than the subjects. When these people are acting economically, they become the sole authority on their value judgments and proceed to act as entrepreneurs directing their energies locally via private enterprise to express their dreams of the future. They learn to specialize and form voluntary associations with others similarly disposed to leverage their efforts and improve their chances. Still, they act when and only when they expect to improve their circumstances as they see them. Since their counterparts in exchange do likewise, exchange takes place only when all parties to it expect to profit. Hence, all parties to such transactions are winners, at least to some degree. Were this a game, it would have no losers. And there would be more wealth in existence after each event than before. That increment in wealth from production is known as capital.

In the large, this behavior, still voluntary but now anonymous, is expressed via systems of voluntary exchange facilitated by the creation money and credit as universal, impersonal tokens of value. Those institutions are expressed via channels of trade giving rise to the phenomena known as free markets. Free markets nurture the myriad, autonomous enterprises that offer the goods and services that gratify every human want and need imaginable by every human person imaginable. And the profits created thereby add to the capital available to create, launch, build and operate new enterprises for more of the same ad infinitum. In such a world, every person becomes an entrepreneur and generates capital of his own.[56]

The bloodstream of the natural society is capital generated by self-seeking individuals, yet it is good for all because, as Al pointed out, "human individuals act when and only when they expect to improve their circumstances as they see them. Since their counterparts in exchange do likewise, exchange takes place only when all parties to it expect to profit. It's as simple as the Judeo-Christian Golden Rule, with apologies for the vernacular: 'We serve others as they like being served so we can be served in like manner.'"[57]

However, Jeff Solomon points out that "Al understood that there are two sides to this coin, namely that a society of free and autonomist individuals would naturally find protection in the marketplace as a necessary component of a thriving and free landscape for humanity. He says in 'Scientific Method,' 'Protection . . . will come to represent a demand for defensive and risk-management services that can be organized and delivered competitively and voluntarily on a value-for-value basis.' He further points out, 'primitive though they may be, the insurance and private security industries demonstrate some aspects of this emerging prospect.'"

This profit-seeking is healthy because it is natural. "The best humans can do is to harmonize their behavior with the world as it is, of which they are part and parcel," Al insisted. "The little we have learned about this process must include the criteria profit and loss, which are the hard-nose terms that man must face forthrightly in coming to grips with nature. To the extent he masters these criteria, he will enjoy expressing his more elective esthetic and empathetic sensibilities. Growth in the understanding of society enables greater success with the former, which leads to an expansion of the latter."[58]

From FEI to the Autonomists

Al didn't pursue his obsession with a science of society as an academic in ivory tower seclusion. He was an engineer, inventor, entrepreneur, and businessman struggling to make a living in the marketplace. He sought relationships with groups and individuals who were interested in the subject and dialogued with anyone who had an opinion on the matter. This started with FEI (Free Enterprise Institute) and ended with a group called the Autonomists. Many of his friendships spanned from one group to the other over more than half a century.

Like so many others, Jeff Solomon first heard about Al through the lectures of Andrew Galambos. "I took courses for quite a few years with Galambos and heard him occasionally mention Al," Jeff remembers. "I knew Al was heavily involved with Galambos in the early days of forming FEI. When Galambos fired his primary lecturer, Jay Snelson, somewhere around 1979, Jay and some other people started having their own lectures and get-togethers. One of the meetings was called Libertopia, and that's where I met Al. He was very friendly.

"Then around 2007," Jeff recalls, "some people started meeting in San Pedro at John and Lydia Goode's house. Al was there, and the meetings were pretty much galvanized by him. He welcomed free discussion and encouraged people to talk. The few meetings I attended were fascinating. Everybody had different thoughts on how to push the efficacy of the ideas that all these intellectuals had learned over the years."

John Goode, the host of the San Pedro meetings, was close to Al much of his life. "We're the same age and had a lot in common," John remarked. "I met Al in 1961. I was introduced to him by one of his neighbors, Leonard Sterns.

Leonard and Al were responsible for my transition from a committed government lover and socialist to a free market libertarian. Leonard insisted I sign up to hear Al when he was teaching Galambos's course. I spent many long evenings with Al at a motel in Torrance, California, listening to the lectures of V50 and becoming familiar with the teaching of Galambos. He was an astrophysicist and Al was heavily into physics, so they were on the same wavelength as far as science goes. But as time went on, Al felt that Galambos was getting more into the ideological aspect of developing a proper science of society whereas Al was more interested in applying the scientific method to society.

"For many years we used to meet for lunch and discussion," John continued, "then in late 2007 we started meeting quarterly at my house. We had some incredibly great discussions about books we'd read. The group included Al, his daughter Rosie, Allen McDaniels, Leonard Sterns, Chas Holloway, John and Marilyn Imig, Peter Bos, and quite a few others. We met for more than a decade, but some tensions eventually developed and the group broke up in 2018. Al, Rosie, Leonard, the Imigs, myself, and others continued to get together occasionally for discussions. COVID-19 came along the next year, and we started meeting via Zoom. We still meet every month."

Although the Science of Freedom Foundation didn't last, Al credited his SFF colleagues for their influence on his thinking and writing, "especially writer-editor Richard Boren, engineer John Imig, anthropologist Spencer MacCallum, physician Allen McDaniels and my daughter, professional linguist Rosamina Lowi, Ph.D., for their generous and capable editorial assistance and valuable suggestions for this monograph ["Constructing a Science of Society"]. The periodic gatherings of the fellows of the SFF under the auspices of hosts John and Lydia Goode and president Peter B. Bos have also been very opportune and stimulating in the conduct of the work involved."[59]

In 2018, Al wrote an essay called "Autonomy" that gave more background on the group. Its original purpose was

> to study the prospects of a science of society. When the group was formalized and incorporated as a nonprofit foundation, it was named the Science of Freedom Foundation without much discussion or notice that the group's purpose would be changing. With the rebirth of the group, the original purpose can be revived and named appropriately. . . . Such names as democrat, republican, liberal, conservative, libertarian, anarchist (no rule), capitalist, individualist, objectivists, volitionists, voluntaryists, etc., were dismissed out of hand because individuals like us are devoted not only to living free of the arbitrary regimentations of political government but also of the stereotypes inflicted by users of monikers of class and group affiliation. After some reflection, I suggested the term "autonomy," or derivations thereof, would perhaps provide a suitable name for our group because it is operationally descriptive of the unifying principle of our group—laissez faire. I rather like being identified as an "autonomist" or "autonomite." [It] invites discussion.[60]

Armchair Quarterbacks?

Alvin and the Autonomists—this would be a great name for a rock band—spent a lot of time and mental energy discussing society, but they didn't participate in the political process that governed it. They weren't reformers or revolutionaries; some would say they were just armchair quarterbacks, criticizing the coaches and players from the smug comfort of their living rooms.

Al gave the following explanation for remaining aloof in his essay "Abstention Is Not Apathy," which is abridged in part two of this book:

> Humans are free agents who need to know that it is their broad and active indulgence in the political system that, perhaps inadvertently, provides the essential sanction of a process, the sole purpose of which is to subject them to conquest like cattle. When they find they are being treated as cattle rather than free men, they should realize how their diminished status is a consequence of their having become cow-like in their approach to politics. Queuing up at the polls at election time bears a strong resemblance to a gathering of the herd at a dip trench at branding time. . . . Once a person recognizes politics is a game and that it is a game in which only politicians can be winners and everyone else must lose, he will get out of the game for self-preservation. This game like all games cannot be played without willing losers. While this game cannot be stopped merely by some who refuse to play it, the

non-participants can at least know the game is absurd and turn off to it.[61]

He elaborated on this line of thinking in his essay "Government Protection":

To participate in politics is to submit to conquest. The sinister genius of the political ruler consists in his ideological coup d'état by means of which sufficient numbers of people volunteer for servitude. Curiously, people are persuaded in numbers to abandon their inherited autonomy in favor of a promise of protection from the forces of nature without effort on their part. The prospect is enchanting, to say the least. So perhaps the politician is not so much the genius as the opportunist. Conquest by plebiscite differs from military conquest in that the former is bloodless and volitional. The victims sanction their own servitude and then cooperate in their own regimentation.[62]

Al would agree with Mark Twain's view: "The government is merely a servant, merely a temporary servant; it cannot be its prerogative to determine what is right and what is wrong, and decide who is a patriot and who isn't. Its function is to obey orders, not originate them."

Throughout his life, Al's main protagonist in the arena of political thought was his brother Ted. Dan Ferguson was a graduate student of Ted's at Cornell, where he met Ted's daughter, Anna. They later married, and Dan got to know the Lowi family. "Al was very important in Ted's intellectual development," Dan observes. "In fact, *The End of Liberalism*, Ted's magnum opus, was dedicated to Al. But in terms of political philosophy, they had a parting of the ways at some point. As I got to know Al a little better and understand a bit of their conflicts, I became an informal interlocutor because I understood Al's libertarianism and Ted's political science.

"Al believed politics had ruined everything and that if we could just avoid it or leave it out, we'd be better off. And Ted would say, 'Al, that's utopian. Politics is a human condition. Two guys in a room can make an exchange, but you put three guys in a room, and two of them are trying to figure out how to screw the other one. That's politics!' Al and Ted's struggle in a nutshell was, how do you conduct a decent human society, which is susceptible to politics, without the pathologies of politics? Al thought there was a way, and Ted said, 'No, you have to embrace the pathologies with it all.'"

Home Sweet/Sour Home

Al's research, writing, businesses, and social groups kept him extremely busy. He also had a wife and four kids, and often a houseful of guests and a boarder or two in residence. His home life was a source of both comfort and stress.

"One of the special things about my dad was how much he loved his family and friends," his son Alvin says. "He tried to have meaningful relationships with lots of people but was restricted by my mom because she would give him hell when she didn't approve of those relationships. Not only was it his work at Terraqua, but he had a social life and spent time with different groups and was involved in philosophical ventures, none of which my mom understood or appreciated. She was jealous of some of Dad's business associates—Joe Galambos in particular.

"I think about the difficulties Dad had dealing with Mom while being a father to us kids. Rosie and I have talked about this and tried to picture how many hours into the night he worked trying to get everything done. When everyone was finally asleep, that was his chance to be productive. I remember him taking cat naps during the day; maybe this is the reason why."

Rosie has similar memories. "I can remember Mom getting mad at Dad because he got home late so many nights because of the Free Enterprise Institute. He would go after work to teach there. It was at Monterey Park, so it was quite a long drive to get back home. He found it intellectually exciting to meet and talk to people. It was a huge part of his social and intellectual life, but a source of much anger for my mom. She was very volatile and could be violent. It's amazing how productive Dad managed to be in spite of having such a turbulent home life with a wife and all the kids he was raising. My cousin lived with us, so at one point there were five kids. Dad was working and doing the Free Enterprise Institute. Then he went into business for himself and had hundreds of projects and dozens of patents. It's amazing he was able to hold it all together and manage to live with my mom. He really loved her, but she was very inconsistent. You just didn't know what was going to happen next."

⌄

"Al's passion for grand theories such as a science of society animated his relationship with people," Bruce Canter recalls. "Al had a real curiosity about people. Anytime he met somebody, he would engage them. He had a natural way of getting people to talk about what they thought and believed. He might end up debating you, but he was gracious and charming about it. He never let disagreements stand in the way of personal connections. He was always charming and brilliant and had a very open heart."

Family reunion photo on Alvin Jr.'s 90th Birthday, July 21, 2019

CHAPTER

Outsized Influence

I've still got work to do.
—Alvin Lowi Jr.

Alvin Lowi Jr. accomplished a great deal on several fronts during his long life. Chapter 1 suggested at least six areas in which he excelled, which are recapped here to provide matching bookends, with the addition of Friend, as that was such an important part of Al's life as well. The chapters in between fill in more of the details.

Engineer

Al earned a master's degree in mechanical engineering and completed his coursework for a PhD in engineering from UCLA. Early in his career he worked as an aerospace engineer on jet planes, ballistic missiles, and spacecraft. "Dad's specialties were thermal dynamics, heat transfer, and heat generation, though he functioned at a very high level in mechanical, chemical, and electrical engineering," explains Alvin III. "He was pretty unique in this, and in a bunch of other ways. The depth and range of how many different technologies and subjects he touched on throughout his life and career were just breathtaking."

"The implications of Alvin's inventions and engineering acumen can't be understated," Bob Benz asserts. "Lanny and I had a fear that his biography would concentrate on his other pursuits, such as the Autonomists and his strident libertarian viewpoint. While I was in agreement with many of his writings—some more than others—we were more interested in plying his brain on engineering matters."

Entrepreneur

An entrepreneur is someone who starts a new business, taking most of the risks and enjoying most of the rewards if the company succeeds, which most don't. Al left a comfortable career in the aerospace industry to strike out on his own. Many of the companies he started or joined were based on, or enhanced by, his own innovations and inventions. He took on the challenge of developing his ideas from scratch into marketable products and services. Although some had the potential for seismic impact, e.g., desalinization technology and more efficient engines, they didn't garner the rewards for Al they should have. But he wasn't in it for the money.

Philosopher

Al once wrote in "Constructing a Science of Society," "History and philosophy of science had long been my avocation although my profession in recent years has been more heavily in technology." His interest in philosophy was an extension of his interest in science. Here's how he saw the two connected:

Ever since Aristotle wrestled with questions of existence versus the meaning of experience, man has stumbled over his concern for matters that do not change versus those that do. Metaphysics is the ancient Greek term for the branch of philosophy that contemplates fixed and unchanging matters, which we can only imagine, such as a first cause of existence and being itself, matters that cannot affect the senses but do somehow enter men's consciousness as abstract subjects that are not concerned with immediate reality. Theology and religion fall into this category of deliberation. Worldly matters that do affect the senses and are experienced as changing events are the subject matter of science, the modern term for knowledge and the effort to acquire the same.[63]

When it came to religion and theology, Al was Jewish but largely nonpracticing. His friend Paul Mullen says, "As far as I know, he was an atheist, but we never really discussed the topic. Most likely, he had no desire to waste time and energy on what he considered unanswerable questions when there was so much empirical work to be done." That's where Al spent the majority of his time and effort.

Physicist

Physics is the branch of science that deals with matter and energy and their interactions. It includes mechanics, heat, light, electricity, and other primal forces. Al was trained as a mechanical engineer and had a deep understanding of the physics behind the products and processes he created. Chris Boehr, one of Al's many scientific friends, says, "Al's probably the most knowledgeable person I ever met, or probably ever will meet. I have a degree in physics, and I never heard the stuff about the scientific method elsewhere like I did from him."

Al's writings in papers such as "The Legacy of Spencer Heath" show his familiarity with both classical and quantum physics and how they related to "nature's order in such seemingly more complex phenomena as human society."

Inventor
"I have over 30 U.S. letters patents in my intellectual estate," Al once wrote, "and many more inventions described in confidential disclosure documents and technical papers."[64] He was hands-on with his inventions. Even as a child he showed a strong mechanical aptitude. "From a very young age, Dad liked taking things apart and putting things together," Rosie said. "I have photographs of some of the models he built and things he made from scratch. He whittled an Air Force bomber, and it's absolutely accurate. I have a drawing of a clipper ship he drew when he was ten years old, and it's unbelievably beautiful. As an artist he could imagine things and draw them, which I think underpinned his engineering prowess. He also had a mechanical bent; he could build the things he envisioned."

Author
Ernest Hemingway advised, "The great thing is to last and get your work done and see and hear and learn and understand; and write when there is something that you know; and not

before; and not too damned much after."[65] Al lasted a long time and wrote about the things he knew and sought to understand. His corpus is remarkable for its depth and breadth. He wrote in great detail about topics as diverse as engineering, economics, epistemology, politics, civics, property, history, immigration reform, gun control, the scientific method, sociology, nuclear reactors, internal combustion engines, climate change, government, thermodynamics, history, the U.S. Constitution, the rule of law, and air pollution. Part two of this book has a dozen examples of his published works, which range from short articles to book-length monographs.

Friend

To these distinctive but overlapping roles I'll add a seventh: friend. It's a word that came up often in the interviews I did for this book. Their relationship with Al is what people valued most. They were in awe of his intellect, but his friendship is what had the deepest impact on them. I heard many stories, like Sara Taft's: "Al changed my life. I was a woman raised in a little box. I had good parents, but they just told me all the rules. Al helped me get beyond those rules and see life in a different way. It was transformative. I knew deep inside that I needed to be opened up to a wider view of life, and that's what he helped me do. It was a very spiritual thing for me because I never had permission to be who I was."

So many other ordinary and accomplished people could tell stories that begin, "Al changed my life." And at the center of the stories would not be Al's brain. It would be his heart.

In *A Pocket Mirror for Heroes*, Baltasar Gracian wrote, "There are four ways to know much: live for many years, travel through many lands, read many good books (which is easiest) and converse with wise friends (which is most enjoyable.)"[66] Al excelled at three of these four maxims.

Lasting Impression

Al believed his work would be meaningless if it didn't have an impact on others or reach beyond his lifetime, a belief Bruce Canter brought out in his eulogy for Al:

> Al was very cognizant of making a lasting contribution and having his ideas and innovations make a real difference He was not prone to ivory tower theories or innovations that had no real practical application. In critiquing thinkers, writers, or "innovators" who failed to exert a significant influence or leave an important legacy, Al was fond of saying, "But he didn't make any history!" Well Al, you have certainly made a large impact on people wherever you encountered them and many of us can testify to the fact that "you have made history," and it is incumbent on us to remember and honor it in whatever way we can.

Al made a lasting impression on family, friends, associates, and acquaintances. It wasn't just his intellect or reasoning skills; it was his genuine interest in others and his contagious zest for life. Those who knew Al longer than anyone other than his parents were his siblings: David, Ted, Bert, Jan, and

Bettie. They watched Al grow up and move on from Gadsden to San Diego to Atlanta to Rancho Palos Verdes, where he put down roots and bore fruit. They knew his strengths and weaknesses and the circumstances that shaped them.

David and Ted preceded Al in death. The remaining brother, Bert, said in his eulogy for Al, "Al was not just my brother; he was the last of my three older brothers who collectively defined, inspired, teased, taught, and paved the way to who I am. I mourn all three of them today."

In focusing on Al, Bert remembers, "My father had a cryptic expression for Al: 'He keeps it all behind his ears.' By that, I presume he meant, 'That's where the brain does all the work and who knows what it is.' At least, that's the meaning I choose to draw. Al mostly kept his own counsel, but you pretty much knew what he was thinking by what he did; like building model airplanes from scratch materials, working on cars and anything else mechanical, learning photo processing, and finding ways to get out of his share of household chores to do the preceding."

"In terms of being on the same wavelength myself," Bettie says, "I'm not sure I ever was. I'm much more to the left than Al, but I loved him. I never got into arguments with him. I knew better than to do that. Al was fourteen years older than me. By the time I was old enough to get to know him, he was away at Georgia Tech and then the navy. Only as we were able to talk as adults did I realize what a wonderful, kind, beautiful man he was. I thought he was handsome and loving and extremely devoted to his family. He had this amazing personality, and everyone loved him. I remember when I went to

Michigan State, and then to the University of Puerto Rico, he wrote me a letter and said, 'I really regret not getting to know you better. I realize I'd missed out.' That shows a part of him that was very sensitive and loving."

"Moving out of the South to California definitely changed Al," Jan believes. "It gave him more opportunities for free thinking and seeing things differently. But he always loved to come home to Gadsden. Mother said he was the most sentimental of the brothers. When he came, he didn't want to leave. He would say he was only going to be there for a few days, and it would be three or four weeks until he finally went back home. He loved being in the house; he loved being at L B Chemical with David. They were very close because they had gone to Georgia Tech together. David said if it hadn't been for Al, he never would've made it through college.

"Still, the brothers were always arguing to the very end," Jan added. "The last family reunion we had, David couldn't stand it. He told Al, 'You're such a fool! You don't even know what you're talking about!' He just stomped around. It was pretty funny because David was eighty-eight years old. But thirty minutes later they were hugging and kissing. It's the way they were all through the years."

David wasn't the only brother Al locked horns with, as Bettie fondly remembers. "Ted was a political thinker and writer. He was a professor at Cornell and the president of the Political Science Association. He was recognized around the world. Ted was an ultraliberal; Al was an ultraconservative. There was no way they would ever come together, but there was a mutual respect. They truly loved each other, but it was best for them not to get into debates, because neither one was going to win. Still, I think they enjoyed the intellectual exercise."

Jan agrees. "My siblings were strong people with strong opinions. It was in the blood. It was promoted in our home. You could talk till you were blue in the face and Al wouldn't change his mind, yet he was also so kind and sweet. He was a very loving person. When we'd talk on the phone, he was so happy to hear my voice. It makes me just miss him."

Al and Mina had four children: Rosamina, Edna, Alvin III, and David, Mina's son from a previous marriage, whom Al adopted. Rosie and Alvin were available to contribute to this biography. Their memories shared throughout this book show the love and respect they had for their father. They witnessed his challenges, successes, and failures firsthand, which only deepened their appreciation for him.

"One of the things that's special about my dad was how much he loved his family and friends," Alvin mused. "You can see it in the stories recounted in these pages. Some of them are not positive, but they still show him trying to navigate life and have deep relationships with people he cared about. That was such a big part of who he was."

Agreeing wholeheartedly with her brother, Rosie added: "There was nothing my dad liked better than to be with family and friends. He loved gatherings of all sorts and didn't need a formal occasion to get everyone together for a meal, a bottle of wine, a chin-wag, and a music recital of some kind. His enthusiasm for connecting with people and with life infected everyone he met and loved. This, coupled with his passion for his work and curiosity about the world, made him a very special person indeed."

The next generation to come along, Al's nieces, nephews, and grandchildren, also loved and respected him. "My uncle Al was a brilliant genius," his niece Leslie Cosby says. "Nobody I've ever had in my life was as smart as he was. And he was kind and fun to be around and always teaching. Whenever we would talk, he would always try to make it into a teachable moment. I never felt intimidated by him, which I could have been because he was so smart and knew a lot about everything. My children probably got to know him better than anybody except for his own kids, and they were crazy about him. They wanted to learn because he just had so much knowledge and so much to give to everybody."

"Whenever we went to California, we always went to spend a day or two of quality time with Al and Mina," says his nephew-in-law Dan Ferguson. "He and I would chat it up and battle it out. Half the time we were talking about science and engines, and the other half we were talking about Locke and Spinoza. Al was very well-read; he had a particular fondness for George Santayana. If you're familiar with *Seinfeld*, Al was what they call a close talker. Especially if you put a few drinks in him. That's because he wanted that connection."

Final Days

Al had smoked a pipe while in the navy and took up cigarettes after marrying Mina in 1953. After his first hospitalization with congestive heart failure in 1999, he quit smoking cold turkey. But by then he had an enlarged heart and COPD, which compromised his lungs and circulation. Still, he enjoyed a decent measure of health until October 2017, when he was hospitalized with pneumonia. "He endured five and a half weeks of hospital-induced crises, including cellulitis in his legs," Rosie says. "He walked into the hospital on his own two feet and came out with a walker. It was the crusher for him. That's when things started to go south."

When Al went home, writing became more difficult, but the interaction with people continued. "He had phone calls; he had visits; he was fully competent till the end," Rosie recalls. "He and Bob Benz had a beer and discussed their engine project three days before his death. Even that last week he was saying, 'I've still got work to do.'"

Alvin Lowi Jr. died peacefully at home on December 17, 2021, age ninety-two.

"Al's health issues were in some measure self-inflicted," says nephew-in-law Dan, who was close to Al. "Al liked his wine. He liked his cigarettes before he quit. He liked his chili. (Al used to say, "I like bread, but I'm afraid bread likes me too!") As his health declined, he was deeply frustrated that he couldn't get his body to cooperate in the way he wanted it to. He made a lot of adaptations to control the congestive heart failure, but it slowed him down for the last two decades of his life—but his mind was absolutely sharp to the very end."

"Al was passionate about any kind of project he was working on," his sister Bettie remembers. "He was passionate about jazz. He was passionate about his automobiles. He was passionate about his friendships. He loved food and wine. He was not a particularly graceful dancer, but he loved to dance.

He loved music. He loved the family ties he had with Mexico. When he loved, he loved with his whole soul. That's what I admired most about him is that he was so committed to the things he loved."

∨

Danny Kaye was a polymath of a different stripe. He was a co-median, singer, dancer, and actor who appeared in seventeen films. He was also the first ambassador-at-large of UNICEF and a recipient of the French Legion of Honour. Beyond en-tertainment, he passionately pursued and excelled at cooking, flying, business, baseball, medicine, and charity.[67] He exem-plified the advice he gave to others: "Life is a great big canvas, and you should throw all the paint on it you can."[68]

Like Danny, Alvin Lowi Jr. passionately pursued and ex-celled at many different disciplines. He threw a lot of paint on a lot of canvas—and had a lot of fun doing it.

The Professor: Portrait of Alvin Jr. for Marquis' Who's Who, 2021

PART TWO
Alvin Lowi Jr. Reader

Alvin Lowi Jr. Reader

Part Two contains excerpts, articles, and abridgements from Al's extensive writings on a variety of subjects. The originals can be found on the Alvin Lowi website, and links are provided in the hope that readers will be intrigued enough by these appetizers to try some of the main courses.

A fitting introduction to this entire section is a piece at the end of Al's monograph, "Constructing a Science of Society," called Full Disclosure. It gives an overview of his development as a thinker, writer, and inventor. It also reflects his collegiality and humility in giving credit where he felt it was due. He was truly thankful for the family and friends who enriched his long life. Although their discussions could be heated at times and they might not end in consensus, Al remained cordial and committed to people above ideas.

These articles have been reproduced in their original form so there are slight variations in style and punctuation and some footnotes are no longer relevant or available. They don't have to be read in any particular order. Pick a topic that sounds interesting and dig in.

Bon appétit!

Full Disclosure

From "Constructing a Science of Society"

This monograph (Constructing a Science of Society) might never have been conceived had I never encountered Andrew Joseph Galambos (1924–1997). I first met him in 1958 when I joined the technical Staff of the Ramo-Wooldridge Corp. where he was the principal astrophysicist. That company became TRW Space Technology Laboratories shortly thereafter.

At the time, I was a Ph.D. candidate in engineering at UCLA, and I found Galambos, a former college professor in physics and astronomy, to be a generous and inspiring tutor in thermodynamics and other scientific challenges in the curriculum. A collegial relationship developed into a close personal friendship with an intense mutual interest in developing a scientific approach to the understanding of social phenomena. It helped that I had previously read the philosophically, scientifically and socially significant works of Ayn Rand, Thomas Paine, Ralph Waldo Emerson, Henry David Thoreau, and Percy William Bridgman in which we shared an appreciation.

As the Cold War was heating up, we were concerned as to how to make the world safe for us astrophysicists and engineers. Galambos considered his side business in insurance and securities to be a start. I thought this was a novel and intriguing approach. Little did I realize at the time how germane it was to my future interests.

By 1960, my rapport with Galambos led to extensive readings of the works of the Austrian school of laissez faire economics and the publications of the Foundation for Economic Education (FEE). Galambos was ambitious to reach the public with his ideas of a free society and how that knowledge was the counterweight to the increasingly pressing communist threat, foreign and domestic. His success in reaching audiences with his occasional lectures led to the founding of the Free Enterprise Institute (FEI) and other related enterprises.

After an exhilarating decade of developing and presenting rare courses on individualism, science and the market economy, progress in the development of the details of a science of society was significant. However, public interest in the courses of FEI was waning. So Galambos changed course putting greater emphasis on more urgent and more popular ideological matters. About this time, I recruited Jay Snelson to join the faculty of FEI, bringing with him greater skill and polish in presenting Galambos' ideas on property, science and capitalism with a more specific and congenial ideological emphasis. Curiously, it was during this decline in emphasis on science that Snelson named Galambos' scientific endeavors "Volitional Science."

As FEI became more ideological, my participation in FEI waned. Since I was primarily interested in the scientific challenges, I relinquished my founder's equity and terminated my position on the staff of FEI. Since 1969, I have concentrated my efforts on research and entrepreneurial activity of my own design, which was mostly technological in nature and closer to my professional and academic preparation. History and philosophy of science had long been my avocation although my profession in recent years has been more heavily in technology. I have practiced the scientific method more deliberately and explicitly in recent years.

During my association with Galambos, I became acquainted with engineer-inventor-attorney-industrialist Spencer Heath and his grandson, anthropologist Spencer Heath MacCallum. Heath was a pioneer in aviation having invented and developed a superior aircraft propeller, which he manufactured and supplied for a major fraction of the aircraft used in aviation worldwide by the end of WWI. Among his other noteworthy achievements, Heath was one of the founders of the Henry George School and had recently published a treatise on "socionomy: a formulation of the organic laws exemplified in the development of society" entitled *Citadel, Market and Altar: Emerging Society* (The Science of Society Foundation, Inc. Elkridge, MD, 1957). Heath was up in age and in frail health by then but I found his grandson MacCallum to be a worthy heir to his work on society having completed his Bachelors concentrating on the art and community of the Indians of the Pacific Northwest and a Masters in the social anthropology of the modern shopping center. His bachelor's thesis became a catalog for the Princeton Museum. His Master's thesis was subsequently published as *Art of Community* (Institute for Humane Studies, Menlo Park, CA, 1970). My association with Heath and MacCallum concentrated on the phenomenon of property and its social implications. It also led to the cataloging of Heath's extensive (unpublished) intellectual estate. I was particularly intrigued with one subject that still occupies my interest: his novel "Action Theory of Physics," a pregnant approach to the integration of physical science.

Since that time, I have worked independently and avocationally on the nature of the scientific method and its application to social phenomena. My three main correspondences in this effort were, Spencer MacCallum, Allen McDaniels and Bruce Canter. This work was the basis of my fellowship with the Institute for Humane Studies in Menlo Park, CA, and the writing of various essays and monographs (unpublished) on this subject and others. Some of these works are referred to in this monograph. I have contributed various articles and commentaries on a variety of aspects and prospects of spontaneous volitional society, which appear on the world-wide-web under the auspices of the Tucson Center for Socionomic Research and the Voluntaryist. I have also written some critical reviews of politics and political government for the Economic Government Group, which appeared in its "Don't Vote" web page. I contributed two chapters of Robert Klassen's book *Political Government* (Writers' Club, New York, 2002) entitled "No Conceivable Reform" and "Abstention is not Apathy." I am also a contributing author to an anthology on "Technology and the Case for Free Enterprise," edited and co-authored by economics professors Daniel Klein and Fred Foldvary of the University of Santa Clara entitled *The Half-life of Policy Rationales: How New Technology Affects Old Policy Issues*, (A Cato Institute Book, NYU Press, New York, 2003): Chapter 9, "Technology and Electricity: Overcoming the Umbilical Mentality" and Chapter 10, "Avoiding the Grid: Technology and Decentralization of Water." I was also an active participant in Stephan Kinsella's Libertarian Forum Google Group and in Stephen Clark-Willson's Volitional Science Yahoo Group, now ProfitSeeking@yahoogroups.com.

Regarding intellectual property experience, I have over thirty U.S. letters patents in my intellectual estate and many more inventions described in confidential disclosure documents and technical papers. I have also performed various patent searches and consulted with patent attorneys on numerous patent application and interference matters being prosecuted in the U.S. Patent Office and Federal Court.

I acknowledge collaboration with my long-time friend and patent attorney, Bruce Canter, who cultivated my practical experience with intellectual property and my ideas on science, its history and relation to intellectual property. I also acknowledge the fruitfulness of my long-term collaborations with Spencer H. MacCallum and Allen McDaniel, M.D. whose encouragement to pursue my interests was invaluable. The reader will find citations of some of their work and collaboration in the Notes and

References of this monograph. I would also like to thank my Science of Freedom Foundation (SFF) colleagues, especially writer-editor Richard Boren, engineer John Imig, anthropologist Spencer MacCallum, physician Allen McDaniels and my daughter, professional linguist Rosamina Lowi, Ph.D., for their generous and capable editorial assistance and valuable suggestions for this monograph. The periodic gatherings of the fellows of the SFF under the auspices of hosts John and Lydia Goode and president Peter B. Bos have also been very opportune and stimulating in the conduct of the work involved. During all this time, my thoughts in this quest have connected often with members of my family, particularly my maternal grandfather, Isaac Haas, my father, Alvin R. Lowi, and my younger brother, Theodore J. Lowi who challenged me to persevere in these studies.

Finally, even though the extensive end notes and references cited herein testify to my many intellectual debts, I may have omitted more than I cited. Hopefully, my citations, although meager, are accurate. But it is also possible that some of those cited may have preferred that I cited their work differently or not at all. If that is the case, so be it. I despair they are sufficient acknowledgement of my indebtedness to my intellectual ancestors as cited. In any case, however, the views expressed herein are entirely my own. I bear the sole responsibility for these contents, warts and all.

_____

First published: August 17, 2018
The material is part of "Constructing a Science of Society," available at, https://www.alvinlowi.net/constructing-a-science-of-society/.

This article is excerpted from Al's 66,000-word monograph, "Scientific Method: In Search of Legitimate Authority in Society." It gives a clear definition of politics and shows why it is analogous to an epidemic disease. Al believed our ultimate well-being requires that it be studied and understood. As he explained: "Although politics is seemingly a human folly, the scientific study of it should yield some regularities in the understanding of its particular domain of phenomena. Considering its history of failure, it is unlikely that science will find a suitable role for politics in government, notwithstanding its claim to monopoly in this arena of human affairs. On the other hand, science may well shed light on politics as pathology, and even if no cures are found, hygienic measures might be identified."[69]

In his monograph, Al shined the light of science on the pathology of politics. He would agree with the novelist and one-time gubernatorial candidate, Kinky Friedman, who said, "Politics is the only field in which the more experience you have, the worse you get."

Politics, Political Science, and Political Technology

From the chapter, "Some Implications of Scientific Method," in "Scientific Method: In Search of Legitmate Authority in Society"

The term "politics" is used here in the sense originally attributed to Aristotle as the art of dealing with the structure, organization and administration of a state or polity.[70] Politics is associated with regimentation of human conduct and is generally regarded as synonymous with human government at any level. Such a marriage of politics and government is a very old idea, now thoroughly entrenched in the thinking of most people.

Notwithstanding contemporary belief in the wisdom of separating church and state, politics is attracted to moralism and vice versa. This is because both must rely on a monopoly of force if they are to obtain uniform obedience to an absolute and abstract code of conduct. The exclusive code evidences an ideology of state supremacy constituting a state religion regardless of any theological content, affiliation or identification. First hubris, then aggression. Thus does politics become an agency for institutionalizing coercion of people.

(Theodore) Lowi explains how political governments fail, yet they never fail to coerce. He points out that fear of government is one of the central themes in all political thought, which he says accounts for the study of government being one of the oldest academic subjects in the Western world.[71]

While the study of aggression and hubris from an anthropological standpoint is amenable to scientific method, infatuation with these vices historically as means for structuring society has seriously distracted application of the scientific method to social phenomena. These vices are utterly incompatible with the practice of science so it should come as no surprise that they also constitute the two most significant barriers to the more universal realization of self-rule under "natural law." However, since life must proceed regardless, people continue to rule themselves albeit with new obstacles to contend with. If this were not so, politics would have an even more difficult time than it now faces taking credit for all governance in human life.

In fact, as Lowi points out, political government cannot prevail before at least two conditions are established:

1. Each and every individual must be capable of governing himself, i.e. pursuing his own wants while adjusting to the wants of others; and
2. Individuals must be susceptible of being governed, i.e. capable of understanding rules and willing to accept them as worthwhile.[72]

Clearly, these are necessary and sufficient conditions for society to prevail without political government. To employ coercive institutions to compel people to do what they are already inclined to do with incomparably greater competence is a bewildering complication to social life, to say the least.

Institutionalized coercion, like ignorance, is an obstacle to human life and, as pointed out above, an unnecessary complication. Its prevalence in human history, also like ignorance, suggests it may be inherent in nature.

It is instructive to approach this apparent contradiction in human nature by resort to an analogy with epidemic disease. While knowledge appears to be an effective remedy if not a cure, it also confirms the existence of self-destructive behavior even in the presence of knowledge of the consequences. In this sense, institutionalized coercion can be considered a self-inflicted social malady in the same way that promiscuous behavior can lead to an epidemic of disease like AIDS. Presumably, an authentic political science would seek to illuminate the causes of such systematic social disorders as institutionalized coercion.

Politics is the art of "legitimizing" and thereby institutionalizing coercion on behalf of human objectives. It represents the height of human arrogance because it seeks to collectivize individuals, usurp their legitimate authority and monopolize human action on behalf of dubious causes. Nevertheless, it is a willful and ubiquitous practice to the extent that people are susceptible to enticements to abandon their self-governing chores and pool their risks given promises of custodial care for a more care-free life thereafter. The slightest inclination in this direction tends to produce peer pressure for more of the same until there is an appearance of a consensus on behalf of custodianship. However, all this proves is that misery loves company. It may even occur to some how nice it would be if they could crawl back into the womb from whence they came.

Invariably, politics establishes two classes of people—rulers and subjects. Since nature does not ordain such statuses, political institutions are opportunistic contrivances that are inherently unstable. They are erected by stealth and they can only be maintained by force. Such force is not only unproductive, it is counterproductive and therefore unsustainable. Political institutions can attain the superficial appearance of durability by exploitation of base human aversions to risk and change. As a result, politicians can cultivate an inertia of tolerance on behalf of a supposed status quo which, once established in the human population, seems to take on a life of its own. A famous screenwriter and director once characterized politics as false promises with real consequences analogous to fraud.[73]

Actually, politics is merely a human vice like narcotics addiction. It is always on the verge of extinction because the habit impairs the lives of the practitioners and that has been so since the inception of the habit. As Barnum said, "A sucker is born every minute," and politics was made to order for suckerdom. The practice is so prevalent by now that it is difficult to imagine how humanity would have developed without this affliction. The situation is analogous to a hypothetical one in which all humans were tone-deaf and thereby incapable of appreciating the gift of music.

There is no escape from political abuse short of perfecting self-rule—autonomy—based on the practice of the scientific method. Fortunately for humankind, self-rule is also willful and ubiquitous conduct that is always in competition with political practices, which, in turn, are dependent to a large degree on self-rule. Thus, politics opportunistically superimposes itself on natural government thereby becoming a parasite on society.

The virtue of self-rule is that anyone can and does do it, regardless of circumstances, if only to survive. In fact, arrogance must be set aside in order to practice self-rule, and it can be successful to the extent it does not detract from self-rule by others. Self-rule tends to avoid encroachment, because of the likelihood of retaliation. Owing to the universal inclination toward self-defense, those of equal standing generally condemn any kind of encroachment. Therefore, self-rule is at once the prerequisite to politics as well as the grand alternative to politics. It will supplant political rule as the veil of confusion is lifted regarding the reality of life and order in society. Ridley points out that humans have friendly as well as defensive social inclinations.[74] He shows how these natural inclinations serve, and always have served, the stark 'purposes' of natural selection by guaranteeing commitment and cooperation just as hunger compels the taking of nourishment. The survival of the progeny of those who manage to live in harmony with nature would seem to favor the ultimate supremacy of autonomous society in the evolution of the species.

Nature prevails regardless of how men speak about it or what meaning they give to it in their terms of discourse. Conscious practice of scientific method improves one's competence in being able to live his life in harmony with nature. That process demands clarity in thinking. So it would seem important that the words "rule" and "law" be generally understood clear of ambiguities.

Clarification of these terms is not necessarily a pedantic exercise. It can be humorous or heuristic. For example, John Deering, political cartoonist for the *Arkansas Democrat-Gazette*, utilized both techniques in a snapshot of absurdity capturing perfectly the distinction between rule in nature and rule in politics, to wit:

> A caricature of the President of the United States stands at the western-facing picture window of the Oval Office with a staff person at his side. Both gaze out at a sunset. Staff person: "Wow, what a beautiful sunset, Mr. President." Mr. President: "Thank you."

An astronomer studiously abides by the law of gravity while he slavishly tolerates "law" as legislated by various political bodies claiming jurisdiction over him. Curiously, he may never stop to consider the difference in the nature of these "laws."

The former calls into question what rules, how applied, and under what circumstances? That is what life is about. The latter is a matter of who is trying to do what to whom, can he do it and get away with it and will he be affected adversely in the process? That is a game not everyone can play, let alone win.

It occurs to some that political processes can be exploited to advantage by ganging up with others of similar interests or grievances. By joining a group and becoming a member of a political faction, they hope to obtain privileges which, as individuals, they could not legitimately claim. This explains in part how pluralism has come to have such a powerful attraction to people. Some short-term political successes along these lines have encouraged the widespread belief that one can find refuge from reality in a crowd. This brings to mind one of James Thurber's pithy morals: "There is no safety in numbers or anything else."[75]

Everyone has the power to cope with nature in proceeding with his own life, albeit without any guarantee of the outcome. No one has the authority or the know-how that would imply to order someone else's life, although physical power inherited or gained through plebiscitary proceedings can be used to exert temporal control and superficial obedience. Empowerment to determine political outcomes is futile because, without a durable connection with nature, the prospects of 'success' in this arena are bleak. Political success is illusory, and the power acquired through political processes is also an illusion.

The initiation of force and its reactive counterpart has no legitimate place in social relations because society exists only among individuals who are normally satisfied to deal with each other as equals. Centuries of political experience have failed to corroborate a single political hypothesis as a remedy for any real social insufficiency. Yet, the trials continue.

From a scientific standpoint, such recurrent falsification of political hypotheses is curious, indeed. It is as if politics, unlike any other human initiative, is exempt from the burden of proof of its claims to efficacy.

Yet, politics is a natural phenomenon. Like gravity prior to Newton, it can be considered another of nature's many human trials and tribulations that cannot yet be accounted for by reason. Although politics is seemingly a human folly, the scientific study of it should yield some regularities in the understanding of its particular domain of phenomena. Considering its history of failure, it is unlikely that science will find a suitable role for politics in government, notwithstanding its claim to monopoly in this arena of human affairs. On the other hand, science may well shed light on politics as pathology, and even if no cures are found, hygienic measures might be identified.

According to (Bruce) Canter, a missing ingredient in the study of politics as a natural science is "political anthropology." Such studies would include archeological investigations into the origin of statecraft.[76] MacCallum's approach to social anthropology is an example of the studies that could illuminate the phenomena for enhanced understanding.[77] Ridley's more recent study is also illustrative.[78] It deals with both political institutions and spontaneous forms of cooperation by applying biological anthropology to explain these competing phenomena as features of human evolution.

Canter also points out that the more traditional efforts in the field of political science actually deal more with political technology than science. He cites Theodore Lowi's "conquest theory of government" as an example of this category of knowledge.[79] Earlier examples of similar studies are represented by Niccolo Machiavelli's theories of politics as advanced in his major works *The Prince* and *Art of War*. These works concentrate more on explanations of how existing political institutions work in practice than they do on revealing the regularities of human behavior underlying the occurrence of these particular kinds of events.

A peculiarity of traditional political science is its inclination to justify the institutions of coercion studied. Such justifications are usually made on the basis of alleged social benefits and have become known as "public policies."

Regardless of the confidence developed by political science in any specific conclusions, any extrapolations of them to society as a whole are reductionistic. Even if mechanistic models of humanity are avoided in such extrapolations, there is no relevance to society because the coercive behavior associated with politics, although human, is antisocial regardless of how it was applied.

Notwithstanding reductionistic error, the expertise of political scientists has inclined them to formulate public policy initiatives in league with political activists in need of "programs" to advance their candidacies to rule. Since the very idea of public policy presumes the legitimacy of public institutions of coercion, such endeavors by political scientists evidence an abandonment of their scientific profession and an induction into political service, the subject matter of their studies. Then they become meddlers in the affairs of nature, which is beyond the scope of the authority of the political scientist. Not only does this activity spoil his scientific work from the effects of indeterminacy, the scientist becomes a carrier of the infectious social disease that he is studying.

It is one thing for to Machiavelli to explain how his "prince" gains and maintains political dominance. It is yet another thing to advocate despotism as a humane system. Thus, only a John Brown, a Hitler, a Stalin, an opportunistic Mafioso or some other would-be surrogate for "God Almighty" would consider the implementation of such knowledge a wise thing to do. Men of this ilk are like prize fighters who care only to 'win' at the expense of another person. Such gladiators would not even climb into the ring if they cared what their faces looked like afterward. However, it is the experience of such men in history that has provided the political scientists their laboratory. Therefrom, an abundance of data has been produced.

The absurdity of politics as a social agency is evident in its version of the golden rule. The modern statement of this political paradigm is due to Murphy: "He who has the gold makes the rules." It takes no more than a casual look at political parties and their patrons to see how that rule works out in practice. However, the corollaries of Murphy's golden rule of politics are the more famous expressions, "the majority rules" and "might makes right." Murphy adds further clarity and context with the observation that "A Smith and Wesson will beat a royal flush every time." Mao Zedong famous dictum makes the end of politics absolutely clear:

> Power comes from the barrel of a gun. The party commands the guns. It is unacceptable that guns command the party.

Mao was determined to make his party and the government of China one and the same. The brutality of his campaign is legendary. There have been few despotisms to compare in terms of sheer inhumanity. It is also true that few political technologies have achieved such consistent results. Therefore, Mao's design for conquest is a prototype in political technology.

While political science has discovered how monopoly government can be made less despotic, it has failed to show how such government can ever be made humane. So the question arises whether monopoly political government is somehow different if there is a plurality of political parties promoting broad participation in the electoral process in their contention for control. Lowi makes it clear that monopoly political government—and there is no other kind by definition—is bent on conquest regardless of party contention, but that the contentions of factions render completion of the conquest somewhat less likely.[80] He goes on to provide this insight into modern Western politics:

> Participation is an instrument of conquest because it encourages people to give their consent to being governed [by the state]. Deeply embedded in people's sense of fair play is the *principle* that those who play the game *must* accept the outcome [italics added]. Those who participate in politics are similarly committed, even if they are consistently on the losing side. Why do politicians plead with everyone to get out and vote? Because voting is the simplest and easiest form of participation by masses of people. Even though it is minimal participation, it is sufficient to commit all voters to being governed, regardless of who wins.

This scheme of politics is remarkably ingenious in the way it exploits the natural inclination of humans toward fair play, loyalty and cooperation in subjecting them to conquest. However, the ingenuity is not limited to concealing the presence of the gun (eat your heart out, Mao). It also inculcates a desire for more of the same thereby perpetuating the process. So it appears that, regardless of all the political checks and balances that have been devised to thwart despotism, politics is a high-stakes game in which the winner takes all and the devil takes the hindmost.

But life is not a game. It is a process in which gains and losses need not balance. All may win although not necessarily to the same degree. Clearly, politics is not coextensive with human life although this would be difficult to discern by reading the newspapers.

Notwithstanding its popular appeal and commanding presence in human affairs, politics can offer no more than a temporary sanctuary from reality for some people at the expense of all others. Politics gives the superficial appearance of man succeeding to conquest over nature and then it celebrates the illusion. This fanciful notion can be entertaining and diverting from more pressing matters. But the fact remains that politics is irrelevant to living in harmony with nature because it forsakes the prerequisites for the practice of scientific method. Politics claims to be the art of the possible when it is actually only the art of the expedient.

First published: March 8, 1998
The complete monograph is available at https://www.alvinlowi.net/monographs/scientific_method/#politics-political-science-and-political-technology.

Another article on politics:
When Science Meets Politics, https://www.alvinlowi.net/.when-science-meets-politics/

This essay was written almost ten years after the monograph that contained the preceding piece, "Politics, Political Science, and Political Technology." It picks up and expands on two of the same themes: to participate in politics is to submit to conquest, and, political government always fails to govern, but it never fails to coerce.

The Trouble with Politics

Politics derives from the Greek word for civics, which is Latin for the art of governing. In ancient Greece and Rome, governing was the privilege of a minor fraction of the population known as citizens.

Political government as we have come to know it was originally confined to cities (polis in Greek). The "polity" of the republics of Athens and Rome were the privileged citizen class. From that usage our terms "policy" and "politics" derive. Indeed, our modern political traditions are merely variations on a theme by Plato.

An authoritative statement of purpose for political participation, said to sum up the views of professional politicians, is as follows:

"(Political) participation is an instrument of conquest because it encourages people to give their consent to being governed . . . (And) even when voting does not itself produce a clear sense of public willingness, the purpose of participation is nevertheless fulfilled because . . . deeply embedded in the people's sense of

fair play is the principle that those who play the game must accept the outcome . . . even if they are consistently on the losing side. Why do politicians plead with everyone to get out and vote? It is because voting is the simplest and easiest form of participation by masses of people. Even though it is minimal participation, it is sufficient to commit all voters to being governed, regardless of who wins."
(Theodore J. Lowi, *Incomplete Conquest: Governing America*, Holt, Rinehart and Winston, New York, 1981, p.25.)

Thus, political participation enables a few to rule many. This is the other side of the meaning of the official motto of the United States: E pluribus Unum.

To participate in politics is to submit to conquest. The sinister genius of the political ruler consists in his ideological coup d'état by means of which sufficient numbers of people volunteer for servitude. Curiously, people are persuaded in numbers to abandon their inherited autonomy in favor of a promise of protection from the forces of nature without effort on their part. The promise is wholly without merit but the prospect is nonetheless enchanting, to say the least. So perhaps the politician is not so much the genius as the opportunist.

Conquest by plebiscite differs from military conquest only in the sense that the former is bloodless and volitional. The result is the same. The victims sanction their own servitude and then cooperate in their own regimentation. Ideally, the only violence that occurs in politics in the normal course of affairs is to truth and logic. Physical violence is concealed under the umbrella of "rule of law" administered by the so-called criminal justice system. Note that the system is preoccupied with victimless crimes. The criminals are having their way with the system. Who says crime doesn't pay. If crime had not always existed, politicians would have to invent it forthwith.

Voting and related electoral rituals are not the only forms of political participation that lead to conquest. "Cooptation" is another. Cooptation is defined as "a political strategy for recruiting members of the opposition for the purpose of weakening or eliminating it." Cooptation characterizes the proceedings of legislatures where the elected representatives of the people receive special dispensations of legal privilege by compromising their constituents' rights. Plaintiffs retain the right to petition for relief. The petition is prima facie evidence of conquest. A more ingenious scheme for exploitation can hardly be imagined. Had cooptation not been invented by the Greeks of antiquity, it would surely be legislated forthwith.

Typically, arguments for political participation assume humanity has no alternative for enjoying private life than to submit to the kind of public order brought about by political process and apparatus. (*Theodore J. Lowi, Private Life and Public Order: Problems of Modern Government*, W.W. Norton, New York, 1968.) Most people are convinced that community and other social accouterments to their private lives are gifts from government. So the common idea of "doing something" to improve human circumstances almost always takes the form of a political initiative of some sort to get the government (somebody else) to do something individuals would never consider undertaking by themselves for themselves on their own recognizance. Individuals never consider politics appropriate for themselves alone because they shun violence, which is the ultimate recourse of political initiative. Politics seeks to legitimize violence by institutionalizing it on behalf of the multitudes—"one for all and all for one"—never mind the possibilities in the real world. Thus, politics collectivizes the population and subordinates ordinary individuals to the herd. So politics makes a mockery of human dignity.

Politics is sustained by a self-fulfilling prophesy: More politics to obtain more government is supposed to be the remedy for all social inadequacies, which are supposed to be due to "poor" government. In other words, politics is the cure for the problems caused by politics in the first place. That politics is mere ritual seems to elude recognition. Political government is the premier social problem because it preempts self-government, which is fundamentally the only real government in society.

Political government always fails to govern, but it never fails to coerce. What government there is at any given time depends on the existence of self-governing individuals. So before there is self-government, there is no government whatsoever. Self-government consists of pursuing one's own wants while adjusting to the similar pursuits of others. It amounts to autonomy and discipline. A modicum of self-government is all it takes for a human population to become a stable society. This condition can be called economic democracy because every ballot is the clear and irrevocable mandate of the buyer through which he expresses his will, his aspirations, his freedom, and his personality. In this balloting system, the votes (dollars) are never wasted, elections are held every hour of every day and the voting booths are the market places everywhere in the world. In this balloting system there is no tyranny by the majority. Every voter wins in the elections in which he participates. If he reckons he can't win, he does not have to play, or pay.

Economic democracy exists without a political overseer. So who needs political government? As it turns out, only the prospective political overseer needs it. Accordingly, a political vote is a vote for the dictator of your choice.

Politics inhibits conflict resolution via voluntary human action, which is the only type of human behavior that is social. To the extent politics inhibits voluntary human action, politics diminishes society. Whereas nature ordains that the best place in society to find a helping hand is at the end of your own arm, political government aims to monopolize all arms.

Political action is urged on fellow sufferers as a sort of self-defense measure. Somehow, safety is to be found in numbers, never mind the fact that there is no safety in numbers or anything else. Clearly, running with the herd runs a great risk of getting run over in a stampede. A solitary course might be lonely but it might also avoid that risk. Yet, there are always other risks. Indeed, there is no such thing as life without risk. Come what may, life is an adventure. Get used to it.

Thus, prudence dictates taking along some insurance. Contracting with a fiduciary entity to share certain risks with like-minded individuals is both practical and prudent. Indeed, insurance is a metaphor for voluntary government. (Peter B. Bos, "The Societal Implications of Risk-Sharing," The Heather Foundation, April 8, 1997.)

———————

First published at LewRockwell.com as "Politics: A Primer," June 16, 2007
This article is available at, https://www.alvinlowi.net/the-trouble-with-politics/.

In this article, Al defines and describes two types of democracy: political and economic. Of the former, he wrote, "Democracy encompasses the social, economic and cultural conditions that enable the free and equal practice of so-called political self-determination. But political self-determination is an oxymoron inasmuch as the outcome of political elections is invariably a merger of voters into groups after which individual identity is lost. So political democracy is actually a form of collectivism."[81]

Economic democracy, on the other hand, according to Al, "is characterized by competition and a popular kind of voting facilitated by money. It is a universal participation around the clock, familiar to all as shopping for the purpose of purchasing goods and services. Such voting is taking place in an arena wholly separate from politics using currency for ballots 24/7/365."[82]

In "The Illusion of Majority Righteousness," Al showed how political democracy has become a sacred faith for many, but one that offers only servitude, not salvation. His hope for the future was that, "the spontaneous growth in the economic version of democracy now in progress is not only fast enough to replace the failing institutions of the political regime—always and inevitably in decline and reform, and decline ad infinitum—but also to satisfy the human drive for progress."

The Illusion of Majority Righteousness: Holy Democracy

Abridged

"There go the people. I must go. I must follow them, for I am their leader." Alexandre Auguste Ledru-Rollin (1807–1874)

Good citizens believe the ballot box is their portal to participation in mankind's prerogatives to shape its future state of affairs in the "right" direction. To them, it provides access to a most righteous form of political participation, participation that is otherwise known as *democracy*.

The term "democracy" came into use back in the 5th century BCE to denote the political systems then existing in the Greek city-states, most notably Athens. It derives from the Greek word δημοκρατία (*dēmokratía*) "rule of the people", which combines the words δῆμος (*dêmos*) "people" and κράτος (*kratos*) "power" or "rule."

There are known to be two main variations of democracy. The most familiar is the political form mentioned above. It is an ardently held belief that says all humans have a right to vote in the determination of their fate at the hands of their leaders, and that to be denied such participation is immoral. Although the ballot-box act is nothing more than a ritual, the slightest official gesture toward restricting or regimenting it is regarded as a dehumanization of the all-inclusive "masses."

The architects of the original American government were wary of political democracy, which was the only kind that was known to have been experienced historically. Thomas Jefferson and James Madison believed democracy was tantamount to the anathema "mob rule," to be circumvented at all costs by such measures as federalism and republicanism. Such measures as were incorporated in the Constitution were sufficiently effective for enough time to allow the emergence of an alternative, natural form of democracy, namely economic democracy. This form, unknown in antiquity, has quietly emerged under a modicum of political *laissez faire* as the way of life for most Americans. Even though many Americans cannot even spell "democracy," this economic version of it accounts for the coveted "American Dream." Although virtually subliminal, economic democracy goes on and grows even as the garish political form pretends to rule, captures all the publicity and claims all the credit. It is a virtually universal belief that democracy is the answer to all the world's problems. Curiously, the substance for this belief is due to the unconscious form of democracy practiced daily in the marketplace. The political form glorified in public forums is every bit the abomination declared by Jefferson and Madison.

Back in 1917 after decades of aggressive promotion of progressivism, President Woodrow Wilson took the country to war in a foreign land with great popular approval under the mantra "to make the world safe for democracy." But whatever form of democracy was implied, Wilson had surreptitiously embraced a purer form of political democracy for this country, a departure from the republicanism and federalism then extant in America. Wilson associated Jacobinism with liberalism, and, ever since, unmitigated political democracy has gained popularity and moved the country away from the vision of its Founders. Except for a few constitutional cranks, skeptics, voluntaryists, libertarians, capitalists, individualists and anarchists, most people have come to adore the political notion of democracy. The popular election of senators and the corruption of the editorial college on the presidential election are exemplary.

It is a mystery how so many people have become imbued with the idea that political democracy enables them to ensure their prosperity, security and posterity. Circumstances and history fail to support such a belief. Nevertheless, substantiated or not, this belief underlies the faith of the masses in political democracy, which is now more a theology than it ever was a dependable social technology. Churches aghast at the competition shun this rival theology at great risk of losing their following. They have joined the crusade for "social justice," whatever that is.

According to the tenets of this secular theology, ordinary people can become parties to a clique with a divine sanction to act

with intentions to improve the lives of everybody and the institutions they patronize. Presumably, they expect to get their
authority to take such initiative by counting noses or equivalent democratic procedure. For most, they merely act out
this mission merely by allowing their noses to be counted in a
periodic ritual. Every so often, this ritual becomes a national
pastime and a chance to remake the world in their image.

Seemingly, all these well-intentioned souls have to do to become god's little helpers in the world's salvation is to join a congregation of their kind from time-to-time and line up to form
a majority consensus in favor of currently fashionable government policies and practices that would be applied to all, come
what may. These people confirm their faith in the omniscience
of this majority consensus *ipso facto*, which provides the charter
for supreme political democracy. Jefferson would be aghast.

. . .

The allure of the democratic regimen prompted a legendary
critic of democracy to remark, "Democracy is the theory that
the common people know what they want, and deserve to
get it good and hard."[83] Mencken also observed most astutely
that "Democracy is a pathetic belief in the collective wisdom
of individual ignorance." "Pathetic" is a good choice of words
to describe a belief in such an obvious fallacy as a brainless
collective with wisdom. Actually, no matter how brilliant
individual voters, the majority consensus that is supposed to
reflect the collective wisdom will be no smarter than the lowest
common denominator of individual opinion of whoever that
poor bloke might be. It could be even worse considering

how the opinions of the gullible masses can be shaded by ubiquitous propaganda not of their own making. Such weak judgment is even more pathetic when it is recognized that the consensus pretends to be "heroic" and "omniscient."

A clue to understanding how people came to believe in the omnipotence of political democracy may be found in an examination of political participation itself. As one scholar describes it:[84]

> . . . [Political] participation is an instrument of conquest because it encourages people to give their consent to being governed . . . [And] even when voting does not itself produce a clear sense of public willingness, the purpose of participation is nevertheless fulfilled because . . . deeply embedded in the people's sense of fair play is the principle that those who play the game must accept the outcome . . . even if they are consistently on the losing side. Why do politicians plead with everyone to get out and vote? It is because voting is the simplest and easiest form of participation by masses of people. Even though it is minimal participation, it is sufficient to commit all voters to being governed, regardless of who wins.

Clearly, political participation enables a few to rule many, which is recognized in the official motto of the United States: *E Pluribus Unum.* Thus, to participate in politics is to submit to conquest. Democracy merely makes the job more facile, accessible and universal via political participation. To participate in politics is to volunteer for servitude.

. . .

Political democracy is easily seen to be a form of conquest. Participation via the plebiscite is the process. The outcome of the plebiscite is conquest *fait accompli*. The plebiscite has become the would-be dictators' overwhelming preference in *modus operandi*. Differing from military conquest by being bloodless and volitional, it allows the victor the superficial appearance of being a hale fellow well met with nothing but altruistic motives.

So, if there is no vote, there is no plebiscite. No plebiscite means there was no ballot-box participation and, therefore, no conquest. Of course, there are other forms of political participation, it is just that the ballot-box type is the easiest. So without ballot-box participation, the erstwhile victims escape the easy opportunity to sanction their own servitude and cooperate in their own regimentation, if only inadvertently or unconsciously.

In passing up the opportunity to participate in politics, people lose nothing but their chains, which were never becoming of their inherited freedom. And in passing on the perverse activity, they are also spared much waste of time on and anguish over futile gestures. The politically afflicted individual can reassert his autonomy any time he pleases by abstaining from political participation. But such habitual participants may well anguish over such a decision inasmuch as it will appear to their afflicted peers as an act of irresponsibility and disrespect for order. But quite the opposite, a renunciation of faith in political democracy implies a recognition of the supremacy and regularity of nature in all things. This is an essential step for a subject to take to recover his freedom and sanity, and begin to enjoy a life evolving in the natural order of things. When there are sufficient abstentions to depress the voter turnout to the point of questioning the legitimacy of the use of force, the plebiscite will have been defeated. No longer will it be true that no matter who was elected, the government always gets in. Then, evolution of human freedom can proceed at its optimum pace as the natural phenomenon it is.

Ideally, the only violence that occurs in politics in the normal course of affairs is to truth and logic. Physical violence is concealed under a ritual "rule of law" administered by an arbitrary "criminal justice system" that tries to conceal its barbaric retributive nature and its criminalities in the pursuit of an unattainable—justice. Such primitive institutions are typically legislated by the representatives of the political participants who have presumed the "sacred" democratic authority to make laws and enforce them as though endowed with supernatural powers. It never occurs to these lawmakers that law is discovered, not made, and that a bad man-made "law" is worse than no such "law."

The ballot box is a monument to an imaginary consensus consisting of a far-fetched agreement among a majority of the mass heeding the call to the polls. Idealists worship at this shrine, which belongs to a god they call "democracy." This god is a jealous god, one to be feared, like *Yahweh* in the Old Testament, which describes His powers as not to be examined or trifled with by mere mortals. They are to accept His decisions at face value (however perceived) and to obey them unquestionably. This is political democracy, which differs from faith in Yahweh in that it has not yet taken on anthropomorphic representations and its commands can be redressed at the next election. Otherwise, the kinship is unmistakable. Both are monotheistic and universal as described in the Bible.

. . .

The voting majority that underlies the sacred political democracy is presumed to be independent and dispassionately informed. Their sources of information are represented to be an unregimented public media staffed by professional journalists devoted to scrupulous truth-seeking without personal bias, which would qualify their reporting as "objective." If true, the voters would be persuaded only by the facts of life as provided by journalists endowed with supernatural powers to know objective truth on sight. But, to the contrary, the voters are systematically exposed to heavily biased persuasion via covert indoctrination, not only by alien interests but also by their domestic sources of information. Such corruption would be the ultimate sacrilege.

But are the voters blameworthy? Yes, but not as individuals. Individually, the ballot casters are no more responsible for the consequences of their votes than are individual sheep for the predicament of the herd. Responsibility depends on the existence of ownership, the only source of legitimate authority.

Ownership or proprietorship is a strictly individual human trait that is associated with the social institution of property, which disappears in a collective. Political participation is herd-like, collective, and more animal than human. Since humans never lose their atavistic animal origins, they remain susceptible to falling back into herd-like behavior, which they own *en mass*. Then, they cannot escape blame as a class for atrocities committed during a stampede of the herd. But herds are vestiges of animal behavior and animals will be animals— not blameworthy for acting naturally.

On the other hand, individual humans are inclined toward autonomy. They succumb to stampedes only when collectivized and herded or caught off guard in the path of such. Blame the residual animal instinct that comes to play in groups and herds. Recall the conviction of the Germans for the crimes of the Nazis. Since individual German civilians were innocent of genocide, dare we blame democracy for empowering the Nazis? [85] It was a stretch for the Nuremburg Court to convict the red-handed officials of the Nazi regime.

Thus, the so-called democratic decision of "the people," symbolized by the ballot box, is evidence against the crowd that sanctioned and excused the atrocity. It is an indictment of mass action uninformed by science and humanity. The size of the crowd has little to do with the magnitude of the charges and none at all regarding the guilt. And no matter what the count, there is always sufficient authority to commandeer the lives of others: the majority is the might and the might makes it "right."

Democracy provides an opportunity for crafty politicians to create a monopoly of force for the "right" to prevail. Plurality matters only insofar as it indicates which part of the mass is instrumental in the establishment of coercive power over all and which is to blame for legitimizing the leadership and its faulty policies.

. . .

Curiously, even if the majority faction dwindles down and never thereafter becomes but a minor fraction of the population, what it "says" still goes, so says the conventional wisdom. Never mind when the vaunted majority was supposed to have rendered any particular verdict. It must be running according to the faith because the majority is mindless and mute without its leader (literally true biologically). And the majority may never represent an actual majority, let alone a unanimity of all those effected by the policies to be sanctioned.

But as faith will have it, somehow, the political ritual, even if barely intimated, legitimizes the authority of whoever succeeds to the speakership for the majority that is assumed to be ruling over all. How else could the masses come to symbolize such power but as an act of faith. But how unlike humanity as a population of autonomous individuals, sovereigns in their own estates but morally powerless over others except in self-defense.

To attribute omniscience to a majority of the masses is absurd. It becomes outrage when pluralities fall to just a minute fraction of the population affected. This condition exists more often than not. In actuality, the "majority," regardless of its proportion of the population, is merely the invention of a clique bent on conquest.

The perversity of the "might makes right" mantra becomes obvious as the "majority" sanctions its spokesmen to muster superior physical might to dominate and regiment the population, suppressing minority dissent as it goes. Thereby, leaders of the "majority" obtain the superficial appearance of being in the right, which is their *raison d'état*. Democracy provides the means for creating the "moral majority," the leadership of which becomes the "moral authority."

. . .

Meanwhile, a paradigm of genuine social life is found to be quietly evolving spontaneously within the same population. This manner of living is being embraced spontaneously by autonomous individuals comprising the greater fraction of the population. It is the natural inclination of them who aim not only to survive but advance and prosper. No doubt rooted in pre-Norman England where the covenant of private property originally evolved, it expanded by leaps and bounds after the American Revolution.

The thinkers of the Scottish Enlightenment were the first to realize its existence and to inquire into the nature of what has come to be called the market economy, a spontaneous type of natural order familiar to students of the hard sciences such as physics and biology.[86] In 1767, the sociologist and historian Adam Ferguson (1723–1816), a colleague of Adam Smith, described the phenomenon of spontaneous order in society as the "result of human action, but not the execution of any human design." On further examination, this notion of spontaneous order leads directly to the idea of natural law. It is the basic hypothesis of the studies of the free market economy by the Austrian School of Economics championed by the Mises Institute and exemplified in the works of Ludwig von Mises and Murray Rothbard.[87]

Remarkably, the phenomenon of spontaneous order of life in a human population can also be seen as having a democratic nature.[88] This form of democracy or self-rule consists in the ability of humans to not only subsist but thrive autonomously in a population in which they can voluntarily specialize and exchange with their kin and kind acting likewise. Such democracy—economic democracy—exists in a totally voluntary form devoid of political machinations and contrivances, wherever the political form is absent. This form, economic in nature, has been flourishing all along among autonomous human beings and their enterprises wherever they have found the freedom to operate volitionally in terms of free market production and exchange without arbitrary political imposition and expropriation. It is a mode of social organization in which all win to some degree and is otherwise known under the widely disparaged and just as widely misunderstood term *laissez faire capitalism*.

Now the question is whether the spontaneous growth in the economic version of democracy now in progress is not only fast enough to replace the failing institutions of the political regime—always and inevitably in decline and reform, and decline *ad infinitum*—but also to satisfy the human drive for progress. Such growth in economic democracy takes place only as an economic phenomenon, which means naturally, and further meaning exclusively by voluntary human action. This volitional domain is the natural habitat of man. The market is a big part of that habitat wherein unregimented exchanges establish prices as an outcome. Such free-market prices are paid when transactions are consummated. In that event, curiously, an election has taken place. Such elections take place at will 24/7. And in every such event, the price paid in human terms is apparently always and only acceptable by all parties to it and also productive of profitable results to all concerned. The reliance of this process on economic criteria assures that social survival and progress will be not only bearable but also attractive as the least costly for the benefits realizable. Thereby, it satisfies the most fundamental law of nature: the Principle of Least Action.

First published: June 9, 2019
The unabridged article is available at, https://www.alvinlowi.net/ the-illusion-of-majority-righteousness/.

Another article on democracy:
Political Democracy Leads to Kleptocracy, but Economic Democracy Comes to the Rescue, https://www.alvinlowi.net/ political democracy-leads-to-kleptocracy/.

"On Election Day, I stay home," says comedian George Carlin." Two reasons: first of all, voting is meaningless; this country was bought and paid for a long time ago. That empty shit they shuffle around and repackage every four years doesn't mean a thing. Second, I don't vote, because I firmly believe that if you vote, you have no right to complain. I know some people like to twist that around and say, "If you don't vote you have no right to complain." But where's the logic in that? Think it through: if you vote, and you elect dishonest, incompetent politicians, and they screw things up, then you're responsible for what they've done. You voted them in. You caused the problem. You have no right to complain. I, on the other hand, who did not vote—who, in fact, did not even leave the house on Election Day—am in no way responsible for what these politicians have done and have every right to complain about the mess you created. Which I had nothing to do with. Why can't people see that?[89]

Al would agree wholeheartedly with George. Although he thought deeply and wrote extensively about politics, Al didn't participate in politics in any form. He didn't follow candidates or issues, he didn't vote, he didn't protest or sign petitions. As he explained in "No Conceivable Reform," "I try to avoid letting my nose be counted in any political poll whatever lest I inadvertently sanction a continuation of the political process that threatens my existence."[90]

In this monograph, Al laid out his thinking in minute detail and invited readers to follow his logic to the same conclusions, or to justify differing conclusions with the same degree of scientific rigor as he did his. This abridgment consists of three sections from the monograph. Readers who appreciate the beginning and ending of Al's argument can explore the path in between by reading the unabridged version.

Abstention Is Not Apathy: Must We Depend on Political Protection?
Abridged

Contents

Doing Something Versus Doing Nothing

Typically, arguments for political participation ASSUME humanity has no alternative for enjoying private life than to submit to the kind of public order brought about by political means. Most people are convinced that the community and society accouterments to their private lives are gifts from government. So the common idea of "doing something" to improve human circumstances almost always becomes a political initiative of some sort. More politics to obtain more government is supposed to be the remedy for "poor" government. The possibilities and practicalities of this approach are rarely questioned.

At the least, political action is upheld as a sort of self-defense measure. Few question whether such a defense is really practical. Most overlook the fact that they delegated their right to self-defense to the government when they last voted and they cannot nullify their delegation of power to the collective authority by continuing to vote. They fail to realize that they can have no real defense against an institution that is supposedly already looking after their self-defense needs based on a "superior" notion of what that defense entails. Some Mexican skepticism (roughly translated from Spanish) puts the situation into perspective: "Since when do the chickens on the ground shit on the chickens that roost on the top?"

When human action is contemplated in a political context, non-political alternatives are seemingly invisible. No wonder, then, that politics is such an all-consuming preoccupation and political outcomes are always disappointing. However, as long as such attitudes prevail, the cycle of political disappointments and frenzied participations continues on into despair.

Many people believe that to ignore politics is tantamount to committing suicide or worse, like conceding future generations to bondage. That to abstain from political activity will bring them despotism instead of freedom, destitution instead of prosperity. However, such faith in political government flies in the face of the historical fact that political participation has never failed to bring about a monopoly of coercive power over the believers and non-believers, the living and the yet-to-be-born all alike, and that the only thing that saves them from being reduced to a condition of abject servitude is political incompetence. However, this is the only compensation they will get for their impoverishment because incompetence will have denied them any returns on their forced "investments" in government programs.

A political scholar once observed that coercive government always fails to work but government never fails to coerce. Historically, government has always been at the root of enslavement and poverty. So how is it that government expansion can still be expected to produce liberty and prosperity? Without ever considering this question, let alone waiting for an answer to it, people developed a belief in redemption by political means. Regardless of the contradictions, this belief has become a tenet of "civilized" society.

Some believe so fervently in the propriety of political processes that they act out their belief zealously and condemn vociferously all who doubt or demur. Curiously, discussion of this contradiction in the folklore of politics is seldom heard in even in polite and sober company. Remarkably, it is a subject that remains even more taboo than sex. This observation strongly suggests that politics is actually a religion. The resemblance appears even stronger when one takes note of the rituals and incantations that come into play. For example, consider the spectacle of a president under impeachment and possible criminal indictment for perjury delivering a nationally televised state-of-the-union address containing over fifty thoroughly fascistic proposals to the cheers of his congressional audience.

Traditionally, political government is thought to be precedent to society because otherwise, it is argued, there is no way to establish an umbrella of law and order without which contrivance society is said to be impossible. Never mind clear evidence to the contrary.

Devotees of this tradition seek a certain fate in the conservation of familiar political institutions regardless of the absurdities and miseries that follow. They denounce all forms of nonconformity and they mistrust even the suggestion that there may be alternatives to monolithic government and a rigidified social structure. To them, change is abhorrent and should be resisted. They constantly reinvent politics as a means of coping with a world disinclined to conform to human preconceptions. In its most recent incarnation, politics has been referred to euphemistically as a means for the socialization of risk.

Politics does not actually mitigate the risks of living. Come what may, human life will remain an adventure. Politics can only spread the risks via coercive means and make them seem less pressing than they actually are. As a result, deception and impoverishment are spread along with risk thereby impairing people's abilities to cope with their lives with their means at hand. Then, to the extent risk aversion remains a human pre-occupation, political institutions stand ready to capitalize on the opportunity to apply more coercion and cause further impoverishment.

Unrealistic expectations of protection from risk combined with aversion to risk tends to paralyze people in dealing with their lives as best they can. They may neglect to use the means they have at hand and wait out their lives with false hopes of government coming to their rescue. Such apathy guarantees that the risks they face will be exacerbated and that politics will seize the opportunity to play the part of the redeemer with ever greater zeal, and so on ad nauseum.

Politics makes one thing certain if nothing else—coercion. For some, even that much certainty is better than no certainty at all, especially if they can be convinced that the coercion will be applied in the direction of their preferences for order and security. Then, the coercion would always seem to apply to anonymous others rather than themselves. Even when they encounter the harsh reality of the state, they will have been conditioned to believe that the pain experienced was for a "good" cause.

Politics bears a strong resemblance to messianic theology. Regardless of all the obvious problems associated with its practices, adherents remain steadfast in their belief that the savior is just around the next election.

It is often said that a rational man must enter the political fray to fight for freedom and truth, at least with his pen, else he abandons mankind to an ignominious fate at the mercy of thieves. It is generally assumed that the conscientious will also use their pens to mark-up state-furnished ballots at election time and thereafter to sign petitions for a redress of their inevitable grievances.

Apathetic and cynical people reject direct participation in the political system because to them it seems that conscientious political activism achieves nothing. They are wrong, of course, but no less so than their active and optimistic counterparts who fervently believe to the contrary. From the point of view of the political participant, voting has about the same effect as a supplication to the deity. However, politicians see it differently. For them, it accomplishes precisely what they crave—legitimacy.

Neither the cynical nor the faithful seems to understand what politics is really about and politicians would like to keep it that way. Politicians naturally prefer, indeed require, a docile population in order to maintain their province. Such a state of affairs requires that people remain dutiful in their patronage, unrealistic in their expectations, and ignorant of their part in maintaining the political establishment.

But ignorance is bliss only for cows, and politics may be said to work only in the sense that cattle ranching works. The parallel is uncanny. The hallmarks of successful political institutions are likewise custodial, regimentary, exploitive, and extractive. Such purported benefits of the state as education, defense, welfare, security, transportation, justice, and welfare are merely fanciful expectations.

Humans are free agents who need to know that it is their broad and active indulgence in the political system that, perhaps inadvertently, provides the essential sanction of a process, the sole purpose of which is to subject them to conquest like cattle. When they find they are being treated as cattle rather than free men, they should realize how their diminished status is a consequence of their having become cow-like in their approach to politics. Queuing up at the polls at election time bears a strong resemblance to a gathering of the herd at a dip trench at branding time.

It is important for people to understand the meaning and consequences of political voting. They also need to know the reasons and consequences of abstention from such voting. The future of civilization depends on such understanding.

Can such knowledge be any less important than truth in advertising? What if a ballot was emblazoned with a caption warning the user that the consequences of dropping it into the ballot box can be harmful to one's health and safety?

. . .

An Alternative Form of Voting

In the marketplace, voting can express only positive choices using money as the ballot. Anyone who has previously earned and holds money, or has established credit for such an achievement, can participate in the selection of providers of goods and services. No other qualification is necessary and the voter (customer) is free to cast any number of such votes as he possesses as often as he likes. His money ballots are also impersonal and anonymous. As they say, money has no smell.

Democracy is readily recognized in the operation of free-markets wherein economic voting (purchasing) determines who will be more or less successful. Ideally, and to a large degree in practice, such plebiscitary proceedings never exclude any competitors nor limit any choices or preferences. Everyone's money-ballot is equally valid. Whether green or colorless, these ballots are all alike in the sense that they represent promises to deliver value for value. There are no gerrymandered districts, no privileges of race, religion or citizenship and no status or seniority. Everyone is qualified to vote and to run. There is no such thing as registration. No declaration of party affiliation is required for admission to participation. The election process is continuous and there are no terms of office. Tenure has to be earned every day. Incumbency is alien, legislation nonexistent. No quorum is necessary and a consensus means nothing more nor less than the sum of individual consents impersonalized by a universal medium of exchange (money). The customer is king. Who's that? Everybody!

Adam Smith characterized this phenomenon thus: "In the obvious and simple system of natural liberty, the labors of individuals would be led by an invisible hand to contribute to the common good" (from *An Inquiry into the Nature and Causes of the Wealth of Nations*, 1776). While his publication was too late to benefit the founders and subsequent subjects of the United States as a political entity, Smith's insights are still highly informative and relevant guides to present society. Nobel Laureate Friedrich A. Hayek recently noted Smith's perspicacity in the summary of his last published book (*Denationalization of Money-The Argument Refined*, Third Edition, Institute of Economic Affairs, London, 1990): "In a world governed by pressures of organized interests, we cannot count on benevolence, intelligence or understanding but only on sheer self-interest to give us the institutions we want. The insight and wisdom of Adam Smith stand today."

. . .

What Can Be Done

The existence of autonomous human life on this planet stands as a living refutation of political dependency. Therefore, growth in autonomous behavior will eventually shatter the myth of the state and put politics in its rightful place in the pantheon of dread diseases mankind has succeeded in bringing under control.

Autonomous people survive as long as they produce and exchange peaceably with their neighbors on the planet. While autonomy is no guarantee of rationality, let alone genius, to awaken to the fact that one is endowed with the power to act autonomously will sharply reduce the likelihood that he will voluntarily sacrifice his time and effort on such lost causes as political reform. He will not pay such a tax if he sees it as such. The autonomous people on earth will have won as much freedom as they can get under the "laws of nature" when their neighbors join with them and laugh the politicians out of town. Autonomy seems to be its own reward.

So political reform is a lost cause. So what if all politicians are reprobates and utter parasites. So what if shit stinks! Surely, only a masochist would go out looking for futility and unpleasantness. And please let's not contribute to the Nielsen Ratings of politics as if it were significant. We might as well allow politicians to be the nincompoops and scavengers that they are and must be to engage in politics because we don't have the power to change that. Yet, we are capable of dealing with cornered rats if necessary. At least, we can refrain from giving politicians credit for being anything other than what they are. They are like the ladies of the night. We already know WHAT they are. It only remains for us to learn their price. But admittedly, it is not easy to establish the rock-bottom price of extortion and blackmail.

Murphy observed: "Nobody's wallet is safe when the legislature is in session." Thus, legislative gridlock is cause for celebration even though the impasse is bound to be only temporary. Conceivably, the duration of legislative stalemate might increase as fewer voters sanction the process. This was the case in Franklin's time. It could happen in ours.

Notice Murphy did not qualify his "law" by making allowances for whatever party might be in the majority. If one is inclined to "get out the word," he should make sure he emphasizes that it is the system that is corrupt and it is the system that victimizes him. After all, individual politicians are only human, taking what they can get while the gittin' is good. Let's not make their behavior a personal matter, criminal though it is in the ordinary sense of the term. That politics has succeeded in "legalizing" such crime is truly the coup d'état of all time. That such a coup passes as "rule of law" is an outrageous deception. Don't let this lie escape your notice. Be prepared to show that rule of law, if any, prevails outside the province of political institutions and then only in the civil dealings among people of equal moral standing.

Granted, such preparation is not as common or as easy as it sounds. K–12 plus college "education" presents a significant barrier, namely cultivated blindness. The institution of public education was concocted by politics to be its "firewall" against public disenchantment. The purpose of "public education" is to maintain the wizard's curtain. However, with the advent of the world wide web, educational alternatives that are more resistant to state regimentation have come to pass. Technology to the rescue!

The Internet also offers the prospect of electronic alternatives to the government's monopoly money whereby individuals may deny their funds to political folly altogether. This dream becomes a reality when autonomous individuals are able to facilitate their commercial transactions reliably and anonymously in cyberspace without relying on legal tender. Ample technology is available to perfect a "money" in cyberspace like digital cash that is sufficiently attractive to users and invisible to the authorities to sustain a robust level of commerce with reliability and fidelity. But it takes time and experience to establish the necessary trust and familiarity demanded by a new kind of money because money is not merely invented. It is a natural phenomenon that is embraced by people. As cybermoney evolves and its utilization grows, the political institutions will begin to feel the pinch on their budgets. This will certainly accelerate political attempts to corral the Internet. Maybe the window of opportunity to break free of government extortion as represented by the Internet won't last. Yet, it is just possible that the unregimented Internet has already progressed beyond the point of no return. Politicians may be ambitious, arrogant, and predatory but they are not knowingly suicidal.

Nature apparently denies us mere humans the option of changing human nature. However, it does give us the option of abstaining from participation in destructive practices. While we can change ourselves, we cannot change others. Clearly, election to political office doesn't change anybody. It just perverts the ordinarily benign self-interest inclinations of humans and diverts them into predatory enterprises.

We manage to survive freelance criminality without any help from the state. We are surviving institutionalized criminality in spite of the state. So why not just shun the political bastards collectively? If you are going to patronize somebody, you should make sure that person is engaged in making an honest living as you are. You have your precious life to live and you don't have time for sergeants, shepherds, eleemosnynaries, mendicants, or predators. If you are rational, you won't concede any part of your life to some quixotic scheme conjured up by some clever but bankrupt snake oil salesmen to fake you out. The taxes taken from you at the point of a hired gun are one thing. The taxes you pay in anguish over the atrocity is yet another matter. If you think for a second, you won't do it. You are the new breed, not the Borgias. Your autonomy is your strength. Use it or lose it.

First published: February 1, 1999 at Economic.net
The unabridged monograph is available at https://www.alvinlowi.net/abstention-is-not-apathy/.

Other articles dealing with abstaining from political involvement:
"No Conceivable Reform," https://www.alvinlowi.net/no-conceivable-reform/.

A Response to No Conceivable Reform," https://www.alvinlowi.net/a-response-to-no-conceivable-reform/.

Al had a profound appreciation for, and adherence to, the scientific method as a means of sorting truth from error. He believed the scientific method should be used to study the social phenomena of society and politics for the same reasons, to affirm truth and expose falsehood.

Al knew such an endeavor would not be easily understood by most citizens. He also knew those in power would resist the conclusions supported by the scientific method. "Still, the application of the methods of the natural sciences to the study of society is controversial," he acknowledged. "Common 'knowledge' and intellectual inertia combine to resist yielding to new conclusions grounded in observational science. But this science is not sentimental or forgiving of unsubstantiated policies. It would seem to be a threat to the edifice of established civic wisdom, which, in turn, is increasingly falsified by observational experience."[91]

The piece of "established civic wisdom" Al scrutinized in this article is the rule of law.

Rule of Law

F. A. Hayek's Unfinished Business

Devotees of politics would have the world believe that their view of the world is all-encompassing, that their ends (visions) regarding humanity are omniscient and that their means of dealing with human affairs are omnipotent. An ideal of the most enlightened political aficionados is "rule of law." Critical examination of rule-of-law and how that concept might have become a plausible political objective provides important insight into politics revealing more of its limitations than its virility.

In fact, dignified appreciation for the possibilities of even-handed law and order comes not from politics at all but from science, especially physics. The liberal notion of equality under the law is traceable to Baruch Spinoza. A contemporary of Isaac Newton, devotee of natural science and early optical technologist, his discourses on ethics were based on his pantheistic notion that nature is universal, orderly, understandable, dispassionate and supreme. Spinoza's faith in nature and science anticipated reason would eventually rule in the affairs of mankind. More than three-hundred years since his time, it begins to appear that Spinoza's vision of social order may actually prevail.

Consider the "law" of gravitation. Gravity has ever been an aspect of reality on the surface of the earth. But until its automatic force and effect was "explained" by Newton in a way that could be confirmed and appreciated by others, now more than three hundred years ago, gravity was just one more aspect of the fickle finger of fate. Newton's codification of gravity along with the so-called laws of motion that altogether comprised what came to be known as the "world machine," elevated that concept to the status of "natural law," an immutable worthy of respect, even adulation.

As a consequence of a belief in the operation of gravity as expressed by Newton and others, believers discipline themselves to avoid the undesirable consequences of the " law." However such beliefs are acquired, it seems that there is little recognition, let alone appreciation, for the process that accredited such a "law."

It is often said that high-wire and trapeze artists defy gravity. They cannot but those who survive manage to conform to "the law" harmoniously. Those who don't survive their encounter with it will have conformed to this law anyway as evidenced by the deformities inflicted on them as a result of their attempted nonconformity. Survivors willfully, if not always skillfully, conform. Victims deny but nature has its way. Face it! "Mother Nature" is an uncompromising bitch. One might wish it were otherwise but, alas, that is the undeniable reality all must face in proceeding with their lives.

Even daredevils submit to the rule of this law whether or not they have ever heard of Isaac Newton. They do so not out of a fear gravity or of the proponents of the theory of gravitation but out of fear of unwanted consequences of gravitational effects. They find that to abide with gravity is complementary to their lives and to flout it is to invite disaster. There is nothing personal about it. Such obedience to "law" is thus a form of risk aversion. It is far more a matter of prudence than of morality.

Such rule of law in nature couples the rewards of know-how with the pain of neglect and ignorance. Its operation is virtually automatic. Violators receive condign punishment without human intervention. Retribution is irrelevant. Exemption is impossible. There is no privilege where natural law applies.

It is only through science that we can get such "law" and through education, formal or other, that we learn to abide it, i.e., rule ourselves. All "mature" adults qualify for self-rule and the responsibility that goes with it. Rationality is the faculty that enables self-rule. It is also the basis for the practice of the scientific method which is the essence of self-rule.

Modern politics envies scientific results and would mimic them if it could. As it is, politics can only conduct a masquerade for an impostor to scientific proceedings. Such fakery accounts for the widespread disrespect for all law. Only by consistent practice of the scientific method can the of rule of law as it is known from the natural sciences be established.

Moralism seeks to impose man-made law on humanity without regard for scientific criteria such as those imposed on Newton's hypotheses in determining whether they qualified for respect. Preachments to the contrary, moralism denies the possibility of individual maturity and rationality. It relegates all humanity to a state of perpetual childhood subject to the authority of an incorporeal father—the state, the church, the party, etc. Yet, no such incorporeal entity can possess rationality. Thus, moralism, to the extent it predominates the thinking of the person, nullifies self-rule which is the only humane kind of rule there is. When politics associates with moralism, there results the most abject affront to the scientific realization of rule of law as self-rule. There is no escape from the tyranny of moralism short of perfecting self-rule based on the practice of the scientific method.

Self-rule might be considered know-how in practice. Perhaps this is the only way "rule-of-law" can be appreciated inasmuch as it seems to be the only kind of "rule" that is consistent with human nature which is invariably self-directed for all practical purposes. Any other kind of rulership regardless of the rules to be imposed invariably lead to coercion of some people by others. This concept of self-rule under scientific discipline reveals the promise of rule of law whether in the physical or social aspects of reality.

F. A. Hayek had a similar vision of rule of law but his discourses were confounded by political considerations and a fetish for existing political institutions.[92] Thus he spent a lot of his precious time answering critics who were mostly, like himself, just abiding Murphy's First Law; viz., "Nature always takes the course of the hidden flaw," where the flaw is in the inherent nature of politics itself.

Nature prevails regardless of how men speak about it or what meaning they give to their terms of discourse. On the other hand, clarity in thinking is essential if one is to have any chance of living his or her life in harmony with nature. So it would seem essential that the words "rule" and "law" be generally understood clear of ambiguities. An astronomer studiously abides the law of gravity while he slavishly tolerates "law" as legislated by various political bodies and he may never stop to consider the difference in the nature of these "laws." The former calls to question "what rules, how applied and under what circumstances?" That is what life is about. The latter is a matter of "who is trying to do what to whom, can he do it and get away with it and will I be affected?" That is a game not everyone can play, let alone win. Everyone has the power to cope with nature in proceeding with his own life. Few are or ever can be empowered to determine political outcomes.

In science, rule and law are closely related. It is understood that nature rules (a verb) come what may and scientists (humans) are obliged to discover rules (a noun) that facilitate anyone's quest to harmonize himself with nature's rulership. Here, such a rule (the noun) is the same kind of thing as a law and there is nothing personal or even anthropomorphic about the rulership to which it refers. This is truly an equal opportunity situation without an iota of arbitrariness. Contrast this situation with political rulership and its insurmountable problem of legitimacy.

And then there is "the golden rule." One version of this rule is the Judeo-Christian admonition to "love thy neighbor..." or "do unto others..." This is nice sentiment which has some nitty-gritty corollaries that turn out to be quite functional as well as widely operational in civilized society without legislative imposition. Tolerance and reciprocity are two such corollaries.

Another version of the golden rule is the modern-day political paradigm, also due to Murphy, which states "he who has the gold makes the rules." It takes no more than a casual look at political parties and their patrons to see how that rule works out in practice. A clear corollary of that rule is the more famous one of politics; namely, "might makes right," or as expressed by Murphy "A Smith and Wesson will beat a royal flush every time."

Part of the problem with "rule of law" is in the ambiguity of the terms "rule" and "law." "Law" signifies one thing in science, quite another in politics. To illustrate the ambiguity, consider the phrase "rule of rules" as the equivalent of "rule of law." The former phrase highlights the sort of linguistic dilemma Theodore Lowi has exploited successfully in exposing the weaknesses of the established American political ideologies using the word "end" as in The End(s?) of Liberalism and The End(s?) of the Republican Era.

The phrase "rule-of-rules" begs for clarification of a supreme-ly important distinction; namely, that nature rules regardless but rule makers and rulers are human, not gods, who must run for their lives like all the rest of us. The rulers are merely pretenders to the throne of nature, the presumed source of or-der. The rule makers are merely grapplers with the elusive el-ements of natural order who have every right to be humble— respected for their humility and condemned for their hubris.

Science relies on the possibility of falsification for its attention to a proposed rule. Accordingly, a proposed rule (an hypothe-sis, to be precise) must be formulated in such a way as to permit an observational test of it by whoever is concerned. Indeed, the proposed rule must contain unambiguous instructions for such a test as explained by Bridgman.[93] This has to be a sobering ex-perience for any would-be rule maker inasmuch as falsification and therefore refutation takes only one test result whereas an unending series of tests without a producing a single negative result is required before the rule can be supported with enough confidence to qualify as a law. For some, sufficient confidence for such status to prevail may never be built in which case, for them, hypothesis is all that remains of the proposal.

Science itself is to blame for much of the confusion that exists in the minds of the public as to what is "law" and how shall it rule. This is because science, in its preoccupation with more narrow provinces, has failed to contend with the theological-ly-derived arrogance that "law," whether "natural" or other, is somehow something other than a man-made hypothesis.

Therefore, such attributes as universal, infallible, immutable and unquestionable become attached to any so-called law whereupon all refinement ends. To attribute such certain virtues to law is epistemological nonsense but the practice is nevertheless very pervasive and mischievous.

Academic science rarely discusses its inner workings or method as if to disclose it to the public might somehow tarnish the luster of its peerless image and depreciate its public esteem. Actually, if the truth were known and the scientists were more forthcoming in explaining how they ever expected to prove the worth of their accomplishments, it would become obvious to all that the scientific method is nothing more than a prudent way of life by means of which all manage to continue living in an uncertain world. It is just that scientists have prepared themselves with more sophisticated and powerful tools of the trade Science does have a problem in this regard that partially explains its reluctance to discuss its methods. That problem lies in the reluctance of scientists to acknowledge a basic consensus on the elements of their practices.

One point is clear, however, which is that politics has no monopoly of the subject of "rule of law" (rule of rules). Up to now, it hardly has any legitimate claim at all, rhetoric to the contrary notwithstanding. Although Hayek can be faulted for his inconsistencies on the matter, he was able to visualize its essence if not its operation. Like all good liberals, he was concerned with arbitrary tyranny. He called the alternative "spontaneous order" and admitted he was not independent of Adam Smith on the concept. I prefer the term "natural order" because ignorance is, after all, no excuse. It would be interesting to research how John Locke regarded the notion of natural order and the concept of rule of law in the context of a more innocent but primitive age.

Certainly, politics is natural. Thus, its scientific study should yield some regularities in the understanding of its chosen domain of phenomena. I believe Theodore Lowi's "conquest theory of government" is in this category of knowledge.[94] But the relevance of those regularities of understanding will, of necessity, be limited to a chosen domain of events and whatever confidence is developed to support any specific conclusions will never be sufficient to justify institutionalized coercion on their behalf unless you happen to be another John Brown or other would-be surrogate for "God Almighty."

Should political science attempt to assert its hegemony over a domain of phenomena that is beyond its reach or relevance, its findings will remain indeterminate or irrelevant and any deliberate social implementations based on them will be grotesque. Political scientists, like all scientists, are obliged to discriminate their field of study to accord with their methods and means, and vice versa. They are no less subservient to observational discipline than any other scientists, or anyone else for that matter. Otherwise, they will be like the guy who tries to sit on two pots at the same time. The trouble with politics is that it leaves the mess for somebody else to clean up.

It's too bad Hayek did not concentrate more on the meaning of "rule" and "law." He was well-enough prepared. He was well-versed in his colleague Karl Popper's theories of knowledge[95] and was intellectually up to the task as evidenced by his contribution to Koestler's Beyond Reductionism.

Not only that epistemological work but also his last book, *Denationalization Of Money: The Argument Refined*, deserves consideration by his critics. But that's another subject.

First published: September 20, 1996
This article is available at, https://www.alvinlowi.net/rule-of-law/.

Money is any article or substance used as a medium of exchange. It's a key ingredient of human society. This is because, "money facilitates cooperation," as Al wrote in, "Money: An Indispensable Root of Community."[96] "Cooperation is the sine qua non of community. Community exists to enhance cooperation and a specialization of labor. But for man's invention of money, there could be no community beyond the tribe. The point of all this is to recognize that money is one of the indispensable roots of community, on par with air, water, sanitation and energy."

As ubiquitous as money is, it's often misunderstood. In this short overview, Al discussed the role of money in the market economy and how it's affected by one particular variant—government issued "legal tender."

Money:
The Root of All Good

The Bible does not say that money is evil, nor does it identify money as the underlying cause of all bad things. The common expression "money is the root of all evil" is an incomplete and misleading Bible quotation. The Bible actually says[97] "the love of money is the root of all evil" I Timothy 6:10 (King James Version).

I beg to differ with Timothy. Money is just a medium of exchange and voluntary exchange is the hallmark of a humane society. Money facilitates human cooperation, charity and the specialization of labor, prominent factors in the universalization of the Golden Rule: *Do for others as you would like for them to do for you.* Money makes such *doing* easier. But for the love of money, there would be little means of doing business in the service of man and even less charity.

It comes to pass in a free-market economy that profits will be made only at the risk of suffering losses. This tension disciplines businessmen to make the most of their capital and build on it if they can.

The science of economics has found that participants reckon their gains and losses in terms of subjective values of their own, which are invisible to others. Were it not for money, exchange would be limited to the goods people could carry on their backs with which to barter with each other. Recall the situation faced by the first European explorers and fur traders attempting to trade with the American aboriginals they encountered in their travels.

The market economy that we may well take for granted, and by which means the world's billions of people live in anonymous plenty, came about with the advent of money, a universal substitute for barterable commodities and services. Money enabled the settlement of bargains in terms of prices, those universal and impersonal substitutes for values. Thus, money, consisting of units of value that could be expressed numerically, became acceptable and circulated as a universal and rational medium of exchange. Incidentally, money eventually enabled the storage of values allowing accumulation of wealth without the need for ostentatious trappings and large warehouses. Thanks to money, wealth can be digitized and stored in unlimited amounts in books of account tucked away securely but accessible in a flash from digitized electronic storage. Such stored wealth is the source of capital, which is the essential ingredient for economic growth and human progress.

The invention of money allowed the development of prices, the public proxy for values. The importance of this development has not always been fully appreciated.

> "Nowadays people know the price of everything and the value of nothing."
> — Oscar Wilde, *The Picture of Dorian Gray*

Oscar Wilde died over a hundred years ago but his sentiments live on.

From pricing systems, we got systems of bookkeeping and accounting. This technology facilitated a high degree of precision in keeping track of profits and losses, assets and liabilities, such that an entity could manifest its trust-worthiness in trading (money issue) and its credit worthiness for transactions in lieu of accumulated funds. This phenomenon gave rise to the institutions of insurance, finance, banking and trusts, savings and loans, etc. It also played a role in the rise of publicly-owned firms issuing shares of undivided ownership that are qualified to trade in public markets where large amounts of capital can be raised from large numbers of small investors.

From the standpoint of the market, exchanges take place upon a bargain struck between the parties expressed in terms of a tangible medium of exchange. Such exchange is visible. In primitive times, the medium of exchange might have been a quantity of some commodity of common value—a trinket or an item of jewelry—acting as a temporary store of value not necessarily needed for immediate consumption but which could be set aside in reserve for future transactions with high expectation of desirability in the indefinite future.

As time advanced, transactions became more frequent and more distant from the parties exchanging. Barter of goods was gradually replaced by money, a more universal proxy for goods and services. In the beginning, tokens rendered in precious metals and such were accepted as place-takers for any priceable consumable. Such tangibles were barely one step removed from barter because they may have some utility apart from a particular, immediate demand or use. For instance, coins have numismatic value apart from their denomination in units of money. Indeed, paper receipts for such tokens issued by banks are not that far removed from barter either, which explains how easily they became acceptable in trade.

Money underwent further detachment from tangibles when the government rescinded the redeemability of its circulating media, at the time consisting of paper certificates of various denominations redeemable in pure silver and gold coins minted by the government having equal face value. Paper notes issued by the U.S. Treasury were declared "legal tender" and mandated acceptable for all transactions and debt settlements. So, what conceivable value backs the Treasury notes? The answer to this question can be found in understanding what the government can do for the specific bearer on demand.

The government is not a producer of valuable goods and services, its productive capacity being limited to printing currency and checks payable in the same. But the Government has a monopoly on the use of force in society, if that ability can be considered a marketable service. So, it must be this monopoly power of coercion that backs the dollar.

Ever since the currency redemption disconnect, the public has been conditioned to accept the government's money fiat.[98] The government now issues money even though there is no longer any guaranteed purchasing or asset value attached to it. Because the government is not a producer of valuable goods and services, its productive capacity is limited to printing currency and checks payable in the same media. The users of the currency being creatures of habit, largely continue their usage and dependency as if nothing has happened. Wiser heads start buying gold and silver as indicated by a boom in the spot prices of those metals.

Government fiat "money" has become a liability in society insofar as it permits the government to expropriate purchasing power from all its currency users at will, i.e., political will. This capability permits the government to tax all those using the currency and holding assets denominated in such without actually knocking on their doors. The fiat policy allows the government to simply print what it needs to cover its expenses to be spent before the recipients of the new issue can spend it. The government gets to buy goods and services at prices posted before new issues enter circulation. All others must face new prices adjusted for the inflation of the currency by the new issues. Fiat money is legal counterfeiting.

The redeemability of the fiat money now depends on the kindness of strangers. But as they accept it in exchange for their goods and services, they begin to notice their loss of purchasing power. Replacing their inventories has become more expensive forcing them to raise their prices. Their customers blame them for price gouging and profiteering while the actual culprit, the government, motors on blamelessly, adored by its many clients.

As the fiat currency acceptors become more conscious of the fiat fraud, they begin to reduce their holdings while they seek alternative forms of money in an attempt to cut their losses. The effect of this loss of confidence in the currency begins to show in earnest as prices of all goods and services in fiat units rise irrespective of the supply and demand, revealing a cheapening of the fiat currency. This diverging trend is evidence of the instability of fiat money of any kind, which highlights the urgency of developments of alternative currencies and the introduction of them into circulation in the general marketplace. Nothing else will forestall businesses' loss of control of their receivables, payables and production due to the deceptive signals they get from the spoliation of the main currency in circulation.

Money is defective to the extent it is not explicitly redeemable by the issuer in comparable items of market value. Such emptiness disqualifies it for contractual dealings, tacit or otherwise. This means a proper species of money should have only issuers that are credible producers of marketable goods or services and can be counted on to produce and offer goods of value comparable to the face value of the currency they are issuing. The issuer asks for a certain number of tokens of value in exchange for his produce, which represents a price. Such a price is merely a ratio of numbers of tokens per quantity of other goods that are being priced in quantities of the same tokens. Token pricing develops only in markets comprising multitudes of such transactions and some means of memorializing such. The latter requirement is fulfilled by a system of accountancy, which is an explicit and consensual social technology. Munro money seems to be able to satisfy all these requirements.[99]

People voluntarily exchange valuables with one another. It's a natural phenomenon. It does not require legislation. Indeed, legislation is what spoiled the dollar as a dependable medium of exchange. Exchange is the hallmark of civilization. But exchange is handicapped without the modern social technology known as money and pricing. Such technology developed out of natural, uniquely human practices begun long ago. They have never been satisfactorily replaced by practices initiated by fiat because the real ones are evolutionary and naturally functional with ease and no fiat is sufficiently informed about the nature of exchange and all the participants to pull it off successfully. Real money must serve people voluntarily entering into an agreement, a contract, tacit or written, whereby they can reliably and easily, economically and confidently exchange valuables with others. It is via the power of a proper money in circulation that communities of autonomous and anonymous individuals are able to form and thrive free of political intrusion. Such communities cannot exist without a proper money. Without such money, humans would still be barely subsisting in family units and tribes.

Money innovator E.C. Riegel had the above cited realities in mind when he formulated his theory of private enterprise money.[100] Based on my study of Riegel, I find a lot of similarity between the cryptos and Riegel's Valun system, which was conceived ages before the technology that facilitates crypto money was even dreamed. However, Riegel's valun money had an essential property lacking in the cryptos. What the cryptos are missing is redeem-ability in kind. Bitcoins are scarce because their source game is so formidable to play and win. Their issue has no relation to any utility that can, per se, attract buyer interest. Valun are only issued by buyers at the acceptance of the producers of the goods and services offered and have value in the marketplace. Producers' acceptance of valuns is based on their expectation and trust that the consumers are also producers of valuable goods and services. This money circle can accommodate unlimited numbers of producers and consumers without any inflation or shortage of currency units.[101] Prices in valuns is an arbitrary number that is negotiated peer-peer with reference to comparable experience in the marketplace.

As such trading and exchange increases in volume, valuns develop a unit value expressed in terms of numbers of the valun units, e.g., how many valuns for a quantity of potatoes or ounces of gold or silver or a composite of such like an index. Riegel's valuns are issued or transferred by the purchaser to the producer in exchange for the latter's goods or services with the understanding that the purchaser is also a producer of market-worthy goods or services of comparable value that will be entering the market for exchange for valuns. A drawback of Riegel's valun system is its requirement for a third-party accounting system.[102] With the advent of Blockchain technology, Riegel's valun exchange accountancy problem is resolved with little more than a webmaster.

It occurred to me that Riegel money is like common stock without government sanctioned dilution. It stands for a promise to produce profitably. Shares are traded in markets for such just as money is now, albeit against the other fiat currencies in the world.

First published: February 18, 2021
The article is available at, https://www.alvinlowi.net/money-the-root-of-all-good/.

Another article on money:
Money: An Indispensable Root of Community, https://www.alvinlowi.net/money/.

"Society is characterized by economic behavior," Al once wrote, "which is the activity concerned with the utilization of scarce resources including human energy with the least effort to the maximum benefit. Economic knowledge is concerned with the minimization of resources and effort to achieve a social objective, giving rise to conservation, specializations of labor, volitional exchange, capital accumulation, innovation, employment, and entrepreneurial venturing. It has been observed that under these economic circumstances, the participants follow certain rules of order that develop spontaneously to regularize the interactions of the participants."[103]

Al believed that understanding and applying these "rules of order" is of vital importance, hence this article's opening sentence: "Economics is the science of human survival." The following three-plus pages explain why.

Economics in Three-(+) Pages

With Apologies to Henry Hazlitt[104]

Economics is the science of human survival. Economics observes the First Law of Thermodynamics, the natural law dictating the conservation of energy, known in the vernacular as "you can't get something for nothing." Excepting humans, the animal kingdom obeys this law instinctively. Humans apparently gave up this discipline for the faculty of volition. Only humans have the option of choice among alternative courses of action in the real world.[105]

Economics studies the consequences of human action in a population equipped with powers of choice. It finds man can and does choose courses of action that mistakenly conflict with nature and thereby imperil his welfare and longevity. In such a contest, nature always wins. But economic knowledge leads one towards courses of action that are harmonious with nature and good for his welfare. As for the global economy, economics finds that the world goes along quite well all by itself, that it is humans who need to understand the world.

Economic science answers questions as to how human social life is sustained in a world where the resources essential for human survival are naturally scarce. It shows that human individuals free of arbitrary constraints will produce more than they consume.[106] As an initial condition, however, they must be free of arbitrary constraints to do so. Humans have the potential to overcome the natural scarcity of their environment with the limited knowledge they have at hand. Curiously, that meager knowledge individuals have of their road ahead is vastly superior to any "expertise" that can be brought down from a distant, dispassionate on-high.[107]

Economics qualifies as a science, like all sciences, to the extent it deals only with observable phenomena. Science has to submit to the Missouri Rule—"Show Me." The problem faced by economists is that their subject-matter is "values" but values of concern are intimate to the individuals who own them, invisible to others. However, values attach to the tangible goods and services produced by individuals, which they put forth in the market for exchange, value for value, with others. That production gets "priced" in the exchange process in terms of barter or money, whichever facilitates the exchange.[108]

Production evidences creative work that is performed only by humans. Such work appears to come forth spontaneously from people acting on their own recognizance. They apparently act upon seeing a chance to advance their condition.[109] In doing so, they are also found to be obeying the Golden Rule, which says people serve others so that they may be served in like manner in return.[110] Adam Smith was to sum it up succinctly back in 1776 when he said,[111]

> By pursuing his own interest, the individual frequently promotes that of society more effectually than when he really intends to promote it.

People behaving economically keep track of their use of scarce resources according to the law of conservation. Engineers and architects are especially attuned to this discipline. When people exchange valuables with others, they seek to gain from the transaction even though conservation may be absent from their intentions. But their counterparts in the transaction also seek to gain, which, in the absence of force, brings the "asking" and the "offering" into balance. Economics finds both sides can gain from the transaction provided each party is acting voluntarily. This phenomenon has become known as "win-win," a characteristic of a non-zero-sum game.[112]

It comes to pass in a free-market economy that profits will be made only at the risk of suffering losses. Economics finds the participants themselves regard such gains and losses in terms of their own subjective values, which are invisible to others. Onlookers seek more objective signs of value at work. They find it in the form of money.

Robust growth in anonymous market activity came with the advent of money, a universal substitute for commodities in barter. Money enabled the settlement of bargains in terms of prices, those universal, impersonal **and** observable place-holders for values. A famous wit quipped sarcastically,[113]

Nowadays, people know the price of everything and the value of nothing.

He was unintentionally "on the money." Prices are not values but are the monetary terms of trade useful for public bookkeeping purposes. Values are private and personal, valid for all humans having equal moral standing. Money, consisting of units of purchasing power, is expressed numerically. It can only reflect relative priority of need in the world of choice, also a personal and private matter.

Money became an acceptable place-holder for value and entered circulation as a universal and rational medium of exchange, first as tokens of precious metals in various weights and eventually as paper receipts for the same in various denominations. Money allowed the development of pricing systems and systems of bookkeeping and accounting in impassionate terms, technologies that facilitated a degree of precision in keeping track of profits and losses and assets and liabilities. This enabled entities to establish their trust-worthiness in trading and their credit worthiness to borrow funds to make transactions without money in hand. These phenomena gave rise to the institutions of banking and trust and savings and loans. It also played a role in the rise of undivided ownership of corporations whose shares qualify for trading in public markets.

Economics finds the net gains made from voluntary transactions and converts them to discretionary resources known as capital. Capital is essential for the initiation of new ventures requiring the personal involvement of an "entrepreneur," the one with the venture ideas and the courage to take the risk. The entrepreneur is the key to the success of any new venture or project. In that regard, everyone is an entrepreneur at some level of risk and gain, even the hourly wage-earner who faces new work assignments hourly or daily without complete, detailed instructions or commands for getting the job done. Thus, to perform the service for which he was hired with expectations that his work would add value to his employer's business, he will become an entrepreneur in his own right.

The entrepreneur's success is measured in terms of his net profits. These profits become wealth and capital to be used or not at his discretion with the consent of his equity-holders. As capital, such funds underwrite all economic growth. Thus, capital is the engine of progress. The timing, direction, quantity and terms governing the application of capital depends on the decisions of a risk-tolerant entrepreneur and his backers. Economics holds that If the entrepreneur and his backers don't have sufficient knowledge to make a success of their venture, it is unlikely anyone does, certainly not kibitzers in government with no skin in the game. It follows that there is no substitute for proprietorship and its discipline—profit-and-loss management—in the economic administration of resources in society. Without ownership, economics finds politics and bureaucratic administration (management by non-owners) incompetent in facing the challenge of making economic progress while conserving natural resources.

Regarding the general welfare of the human population, economics looks for the natural order that science finds in other areas of inquiry about the world. However, economic knowledge is unique in keeping with the unique self-governing faculty of individual humans. Accordingly, among the earliest findings in economic science was the principle of *laissez faire* subject to the integrity of property. This study puts the uncompromised individual human at the center of the inquiry because it is in the brain of each one that economic intelligence is found. This egocentric approach to the study of economic phenomena is maintained most consistently in today's economic scholarship by the so-called Austrian School.

The laissez faire economic regime has been found to be the only way to overcome natural scarcity without disparaging nature. This outcome is the kind of harmony that characterizes science most generally. Such economics offers the means for successfully implementing equal economic opportunity without inflicting unequal economic handicaps. Economics is not a game of winners against losers. It finds no place for umpires, referees or notions of level playing fields. It cannot contemplate an equal distribution of wealth because wealth comes to them who seek it and are able to produce it with talents, preparations and opportunities that vary from person-to-person and time-to-time. Economics cannot change the natural order. It can only discover it. Economics tells us that wealth is earned only in a free and competitive market by the earners; and then only in proportion to the value of their services to others.

Economics finds the specialization of labor to be a particularly significant feature of the uninhibited economic system.[114] This finding should not be surprising inasmuch as each uninhibited individual is endowed with unique talents and goals, which give rise to another inherent feature of the laissez faire economy known as upward mobility. As a result, such economies lack any fixed classes of people based on wealth, income, skin-color, or ethnicity. The erstwhile lowest on the economic totem pole have opportunities for advancement limited only by their skills, health, perseverance, ambition and industry. They also have the widest range of choices as to where to concentrate their efforts to advance. These factors combine to propel them upwardly in the economic order at the fastest rate possible. Obviously, an early start, especially at the lowest rung of the economic ladder, and at whatever compensation offered, is productive to that end. On-the-job training is the most valuable extension of anyone's primary education, which never ends. But, sadly, sometimes, it never starts. None are too young to start. Children's aptitude for learning economic behavior forms at a very early age.

Economics also shows that the rate of advancement for anyone, especially those making the least contribution to capital creation, depends on the rate of increase in capital invested. Capital in that sense includes know-how acquired as well as funds accumulated. An illustration of this economic principle compares the living conditions of a Chinese coolie with an American truck driver. What explains the difference? The truck. And the driving skills. Both are items of capital.[115]

Capital is the engine of economic growth. And economic growth is the key to human progress. The celebrated "99%" should rejoice in the knowledge that the vilified "one per cent" are thriving because it is the more-wealthy among us who are in a position to contribute the greater proportion of capital investment, which benefits all. Figuratively speaking, an adequate supply of trucks is traceable to the success of the wealthy.

An unrestrained economy is the natural human state of affairs. It features unending competition between entrepreneurs, for investors if not for customers. Competition is a feature of a free society. So is cooperation. These factors weave an economy that grows without bounds, at times breathtakingly. It is true that peoples' welfares in the natural economy benefit like boats in a rising tide—they all rise. But unlike physical boats on the tide, economic boats don't rise equally in an economic tide. This natural disparity is itself a natural phenomenon that must be understood to avoid instability from such human foibles as envy. Indeed, most of the political assaults on the natural free-market system have been motivated by the exploitation of envy.

As evidence of its power, consider that virtually all of the economic advancement of the 200,000+ year old homo sapiens' species has occurred since the 17th Century Enlightenment, which relatively suddenly less than 300 years ago, ushered in the age of natural science. But, amazingly and virtually within memory, just a few million humans each barely subsisting for a short time on this planet are now over 7 billion in number living in relative abundance for decades beyond their age for maturity.[116] It is difficult to imagine how prosperous the world's human population would be now had a greater level of economic literacy prevailed to instruct people how and what of their actions and indulgences to avoid to allow a greater sphere of *laissez faire* (live-and-let-live).

First published: February 10, 2021
This article is available at, https://www.alvinlowi.net/economics-in-three-pages/.

Another article on economics:
Economics and Science, https://www.alvinlowi.net/economics-and-science/.

This article explains how property, and the ideas upon which it is based, form the foundation of human society. According to Spencer Heath, "Property may be anything that by the custom of society becomes the subject matter of ownership and thereby of the social, non-violent processes and relationships called contracts, between persons, with respect to its disposition or use."[117]

"Property is born the instant one individual human strikes up a cooperative relationship with one or more others," Al noted. "It is their 'properties' (social sense) represented by titles to such that actually experience exchanges, if any. The totality of such arrangements constitutes society.'"

In this piece, Al traced the evolutionary process whereby ideas become property that can be owned and traded to create capital, "the utility of which is enhanced via growth in population, science and technology," He concluded, "And it is through science that ideas become property subject to individual ownership and control, before which there can be no significant rational social administration based on profit versus loss. The advent of such proprietary administration accounts for all the conservation and progress in the world."

The Evolution of Property
Abridged

It is a fair question to ask at this point whether there is or can be such a thing as intellectual property consistent with the definition of property. My present and most highly developed sense of the term "property" is expressed in the following quotation from Spencer Heath:[118]

Almost any element of human environment can be or become property. It becomes such, not alone by act of its possessor, but by the natural law of custom of the society, designating it under various circumstances and conditions as property, and resigning or appropriating it to him as the owner.

Property results only from societal custom, convention or agreement. Wealth from the labor or activity called production becomes property by the same convention. Property can exist, as property, only in a society.

The social will creates property in both natural and artificial things—so far as it holds them subject to none other but voluntary or contractual distribution or disposition. Natural things cannot themselves be created or produced; wealth is created by artifice or labor applied to what once were natural things. Neither land nor wealth is, of itself, necessarily, property.

Property may be anything that by the custom of society becomes the subject matter of ownership and thereby of the social, non-violent processes and relationships called contracts, between persons, with respect to its disposition or use.

. . .

Property is born the instant one individual human strikes up a cooperative relationship with one or more others. It is their "properties" (social sense) represented by titles to such that actually experience exchanges, if any. The totality of such arrangements constitutes "society." Thus, society is defied by Heath as a population within a population. As such, society is a continuum of spontaneous associations of individuals willing, able and engaged in activities expected to advance their lives via specialization and cooperation as they alone can achieve. Such an "organization" is based on the voluntary exchanges of their properties. This practice constitutes the institution of property.

Heath's definition of property as a social phenomenon focuses on the creative effects individual humans have on each other. Improvisation is inescapable in anticipation of cooperation between vastly differing individuals. In its institutional sense, property defines the relationships people choose to have with each other, different in every case. Remarkably, a consensus is seen to develop in this ever-changing environment such that there must be a basic law of nature at play to explain this regularity under the circumstances. That law, I surmise, is the *universal integrity of property*. But it is more generally known as the Golden Rule.[119] The equivalence is undeniable. Note according to Heath's definition, property comes into existence the instant two or more humans come into contact.

. . .

Heath's notion of property is amplified by the following observation of a well-known anthropologist:[120]

> . . . although an individual may be the possessor of some valued object, . . . that object does not become property until the members of the society agree, tacitly or explicitly, to bestow the property attribute upon the object by regulating their behavior with respect to it in a self-limiting manner.

This observation is a good example of an operational definition of property, explaining as it does how one goes about looking at the phenomenon for himself in an actual social situation with an eye toward instructing others. It is the anthropologist's view that society or community is established when members are found to be bestowing respect and forbearance on each other's property. This spontaneous, mutual, "tit-for-tat" behavior identifies the reciprocal aspect of ownership and connects it with the origin of volitional cooperation and community or social living that goes on everywhere people communicate freely, i.e., without compulsion.

. . . . . .

Only after disclosure can a market for ideas develop. Disclosure is likely in response to ambitions to find advantages in making improvements to circumstances. Such aims are futile without workable ideas for implementation. Ultimately, some ideas will endure the process of entering the economy as a whole with its interminable and comprehensive trials, error-findings, evaluations, venturings, offerings of diverse products and services and exchanges of property of all kinds. It all starts with unambiguous claims to ideas and mutual tolerance for such claims.

Civil society is characterized by the establishment of quiet possession. Quiet possession is an outcome of successful application and unambiguous identification. It is unambiguous identification that gives all property an intellectual component. It may be said that while strictly intellectual effects cannot be property, all property has an intellectual component.

Ideas objectified to the degree necessary to be treated as useful possessions can become property as a result of the social intercourse that can occur thereby. It is possible for ideas to remain confidential as trade secrets, but they must be disclosed to the public and offered up on the altar of falsification via the method of science if they would seek recognition as knowledge or know-how. Bona fide knowledge can never be secret because ideas seeking scientific accreditation must be disclosed to a jury of one's peers whose proceedings must be open to public scrutiny. Such is the nature of science. Thus, a "trade secret" cannot lay claim to special knowledge until its veil of secrecy is lifted and a full disclosure of its workings and claims is made to a knowledgeable jury of independent observers.

Note that ideas become property not alone by the mental gymnastics of the host of the mental stage where the birthing performance (ideation) takes place and erstwhile custody is provided. It is also necessary that the consensual customs of the community come into play whereby the ideas may be examined, exchanged, tried-out and employed independently. The particular customs that develop in the course of applying the proprietary practices that evolve depend on the market and cultural conditions that prevail at the time. Those practices are likely to be spontaneous and surprising, but they produce the various social customs that develop to evidence the existence of the institution of property and induce acknowledgements of priority of conception, custody and use. Typically, concessions of ownership with the expectation of profit and reciprocity result from such acknowledgements. Those societies that foster such proprietorship have been found to set the standards for social behavior conducive to economic and social progress as evidenced by the histories of the respective cultural practices. Evidence of humane consistency consists of growth in technological prowess, knowledge, capital accretion, population, charity, tranquility and lifespan.

Ideas that become property typically carry a chain of recognition back to the originators and contributors of the benefits associated with the first reductions to practice of their ideas. That recognition is most generally known as a "title," short for entitlement to the prerogatives of ownership including the identification of the entity who speaks for this authority.

. . .

History portrays a thankless world; negligent, dismissive or even exploitive in its seeming disregard for property. This behavior is now seen to be contrary to what we now know to be naturally humane and productive social etiquette. It calls for a variety of tangible acknowledgements to authors, inventors and innovators beginning with simple gratitude as described by Woods. These customs are actually quite familiar and unobtrusive. They can be observed in rudimentary form in practice here and there and from time to time with just enough regularity to inspire some to invest in creative endeavors. No doubt a few so strive in step with their own sense of achievement but there can never be enough such recognition in view of its significance in the progress of the species. While it takes ever so long for such humane and progressive practices to evolve under the aegis of the voluntary encouragements that occur in a free market environment, otherwise, it never happens. There is no alternative to freedom when it comes to the creation of human progress. The popular idea of a super-human state that is capable of human reformation and "perfection" is without an iota support in actuality. Its lingering popularity is perhaps the most pernicious vice in human history.

Ideas are the result of irrepressible induction in perpetual motion in the ever-ready human faculty of cognition. Ideas are a uniquely human product, which means that they properly belong to the individual that produced them. Since they are produced privately in the author's brain, they are under his absolute control until they are disclosed to others. Ideas are at least the precursors to property.

Induction is that little understood creative ability of humans to focus native curiosity on items of experience in search of order among them where none is immediately apparent. This process goes by various names such as guessing, speculating, daydreaming, hypothesizing, postulating, inventing, composing, etc. . . .

A person's ability to generalize concepts from particular experience by induction varies widely. Variable likewise is his ability to analyze such generalizations by projecting specific possibilities and outcomes from them via his faculty of deduction or logical reasoning. Consequently, man contemplates a risky venture when he projects his conclusions and aims at future circumstances. Questions arise as to which if any of his ideas is relevant in the world in which he lives. A conjunction of the most favorable factors is necessary before he can muster sufficient bravery to test the projections of his ideas as to their consistency with reality. He is tested further when he discloses his ideas to others. That step signifies he believes with some degree of confidence as sanctioned by his peers that he has knowledge pertinent to his survival and advancement in nature. Convincing such a jury obtains the corroboration and confirmation he will require to break his solitude and enter the world of social cooperation.

The salient point here is that the author of the idea cannot succeed in reality entirely alone. He must communicate and cooperate with certain others if he is to make any history. He has no other choice under real world circumstances. He, in whose brain the idea, any idea, was hatched, stands as the author never to be replaced as such by any other person regardless of circumstances. But he must have accomplices to advance his idea toward a real world event. Since no two ideas are alike, even by the same person, each such effort will also be unique. Like the real world he lives in as a *fait accompli,* the rule of nature is "to each his own"—everyone is unique in the permanent world at large. Yet, he has his *own, but* only insofar as he keeps it to himself alone. And there's the rub.

At the starting point in the history of ideas, the author has absolute authority over his own. This lasts only as long as his ideas are not discovered by others. Only he can decide to disclose and take his chances with the treatment he can get subsequently as only the author of those ideas in the world at large. But that title is cold comfort. It may well be as Thomas Paine once pronounced, that dearness is what gives things their value. And so, a unique life alone with its unique ideas is priceless. But ideas must be "priceable" if they are to bring tangible rewards to their author. To be priceable, ideas must be embodied in a sufficiently tangible manner to qualify for exchange with others. Until then, there can be no price. To reach this point of maturity with any idea, it may take more than one good man's manpower for him to survive living with it alone. If he is conscientious, he will agonize over a few inevitable mistakes, living in fear those mistakes will be discovered by others before he can correct them.

Even then, success at pricing is challenging, to say the least. Here's the innovator looking over a wall beyond which his future lies. He has only his own bootstraps with which to lift himself up and over. A greater futility can hardly be imagined. But soon enough, he gets the idea that the fellow next to him also has yearnings with only his own bootstraps at hand. Perceiving a kinship in aspirations, resources and limitations, he breaks his willful isolation and offers his fellow traveler an assist, a lift up to the top of the wall via a grip on his fellow's bootstraps. But there is one condition: once on top, his fellow is obliged to offer his hands to pull him up to the top as well.

Thereby, the innovator discovers that two good men can not only get by but get ahead with less than two man-powers between them. They will have some power to spare for other things complementary to their lives but not immediately required for their survival.

Note that this spare power is the gain or profit from that very social cooperation by individuals seeking their own ends by willfully acting in concert with other individuals seeking theirs, all without the compulsion of another. Just the possibility of such gain and accumulation motivates a continuation of this progressive practice, which is the source of *capital*—wealth not needed for immediate consumption that can be applied with discretion to endeavors likely to produce gains in the future. Such capital has been called the ultimate resource and the end of scarcity.[121]

Conclusion

The discovery of proprietary administration marks a turning point in the history of mankind. The species was endowed at birth with this capacity to create a three-or-more-member social entity without the application of compulsion by methods that integrate proprietorship, science and society. But those aptitudes remained largely dormant, subordinate to the affairs of family and tribe until this power of socialization was discovered about the time of Adam Smith and the Scottish Enlightenment that preceded and accompanied the Industrial Revolution. As this complementary trio of man's mental assets has matured in a growing population of human individuals, capital has sprouted, blossomed and ripened in the wake of increasingly competent social behavior. That evolution has enabled solitary, one manpower man to harness much manpower to become increasingly productive of capital leading to an exponential rate of growth in the progressive resources of aggregate society. The strictly human contribution of this development can be called "patient capital."

To the extent it has escaped dissipation in strife, intrigue, expropriation and conquest, capital has flowed naturally and opportunistically into developments that have enhanced human life via an ever-regenerative, learning process of self-rectification that is the essence of science. Ideas develop into communicable and actionable knowledge with which to leverage productivity via wider cooperation, wider assortments and larger aggregates of materials and participants. This possibility attracts practitioners with mutual gratitude all around. Immigration and imitation are important forms of such gratitude. As observed by Oscar Wilde:

> "Imitation is the sincerest form of flattery that mediocrity can pay to greatness."

Thereby, ideas are transformed into property and capital, the utility of which is enhanced via growth in population, science and technology. That transformation takes place as the ideas take the form of definitions of valuable, skills, goods and services applied in response to the demands of others willing to exchange on mutually attractive terms. Such social cooperation takes place based on the utility of the properties offered in exchange by its applications and uses. Thus, property occasions the introduction of science into the picture. And it is through science that ideas become property subject to individual ownership and control, before which there can be no significant rational social administration based on profit versus loss. The advent of such proprietary administration accounts for all the conservation and progress in the world.

First published: August 7, 2021
The unabridged version of this article is available at, https://www.alvinlowi.net/the-evolution-of-property/.

Another article on property:
On Andrew Galambos and His Primary Property Ideas, https://www.alvinlowi.net/on-andrew-galambos-and-his-primary-property-ideas/.

This 286-page monograph spans from Francis Bacon, who lived 500 years ago, to technologies as current as blockchain and CRISPR. It examines society through the lens of science, specifically the scientific method, taking an in-depth look at society's intrinsic components, from property and capital to politics and government. There follows thirteen appendixes and more than four hundred endnotes and references that provide even more detail.

This excerpt contains the preface and introduction to Al's "science of society." Those who want to follow his thesis from beginning to end, or cherry-pick subjects of interest, can follow the link at the end of this excerpt to download the monograph.

Constructing a Science of Society: A Trial Based on the Universal Integrity of Property Principle

Preface and Introduction

Preface

An authentic science of society must lend itself to the study of social phenomena consistent with Francis Bacon's venerated method of the natural sciences. It must also satisfy subsequent elaborations of the method to satisfy modern epistemological concerns. Three usually disparate topics come forth right away in the course of investigating the possibilities—inductive thinking, intellectual property and the scientific method itself. Accordingly, these topics lead the explorations undertaken in this monograph preparatory to trying out an application of the scientific method to social phenomena.

Customarily, the three specific topics mentioned above are considered separate and distinct subjects of fundamental significance in their separate domains of experience. In this monograph, they are treated heuristically as interrelated phenomena, indispensable steps in the fundamental process of acquiring knowledge of the natural world with particular application to the social domain.

The overall objective of this work is to construct the framework for a prospective science of society in strict accord with the criteria of the natural sciences. The work itself is mostly an exploratory excursion into the nature of social phenomena and the epistemological considerations applicable to the use of the scientific method to such phenomena. The latter work is based on an operational definition of "property" and two postulates that use this definition. The primary postulate is basically "universal integrity of property." The second one is essentially the action axiom based on the subjective theory of value from Austrian *laissez faire* economic theory. The result is an evolutionarily stable process that is visible in the human population as it is, which is in the process of bringing about a humane, equitable and progressive social paradigm. Individual humanity is the cause. Property is the subject. Science is the means. Society is the effect. Individual freedom is the consequence.

The interrelations of the three primary concepts—induction, property and science—are found to be consistent with the fundamental perceptions of reality by humans, perceptions that occur as a succession of discrete events, which shall be known as "eventual reality" as suggested by Spencer Heath. A notion of "cause and effect" inducted from casual experience is the starting point in an inductive-deductive procedure deemed the scientific method by Francis Bacon and elaborated by Andrew

Galambos. The outcome conforms to Arthur Eddington's epistemological notion of selective subjectivity: selective because particular experience provides the means for testing logical projections for truth that are entirely subjective because they are entirely mental conceptions.

The study of society begins, obviously, with the existence of human beings, their lives and their estates. These wholly, intact individuals are the units that intermittently, spontaneously, willfully and autonomously join, interact and associate to create social events. The conscious experience of these discrete individual humans provokes their notions of a better future, which enter their consciousnesses via a unique faculty of induction—a type of thinking that occurs only in the brain of solitary individual humans. These "ideas" create a personal sense of the order in the surrounding world, which forms their notions of a future state of affairs.

That induction occurs is indisputable as evidenced by the surprising originality of the ideas that are formed in the brains of every individual human being from time to time in the course of his everyday life. Indications are that these ideas are somehow related to his drive to make sense of his experience with reality in his effort to survive and prosper in the world around him. The irresistible conclusion from this observation is that Baconian science is practiced by all living humans as a feature of their natures regardless of their individual intellectual potencies or preparations. "Everyman" is a scientist.

The spontaneous thinking process called induction forms the ideas in the brain of the solitary individual human, which become intellectual property. These ideas are invariably generalizations of particular experiences however derived. Such general conclusions are as unique as the individuals who created them. They come to have the traditional attributes of "property" in the abstract sense of the term as originally elaborated by John Locke. More recently, Andrew Galambos showed how this form of property precedes every other form of property, respect for which leads to certain form of social organization that is favorable for the existence of humans *per se*. This condition is recognizable as "freedom," individual freedom for each to exist in a manner that is true to the natures of each and every person from birth. It is their natural habitat.

Intellectual property is initially the product of induction, subsequently objectified to be observed in terms of its participation in social interactions. Such interactions comprise social events performed by individual humans interacting voluntarily with each other. As a result, intellectual property sheds its abstract and personal origins to become an existential factor in virtually all social manifestations. Moreover, the observability of such property qualifies it as fit subject-matter for treatment by the scientific method. Intellectual property is transformed thereby from merely subjective thoughts buried in the imagination into sensible and consensual factors that can be contested by others and examined for consistency with reality using the scientific method.

In this monograph, property, including the intellectual form, is taken from its abstract definition and put into a social context where it becomes operationally defined as required for the conduct of scientific proceedings. In this form, property can be contemplated not merely as an abstract and psychological construct but also as a natural social phenomenon. It was Spencer Heath who showed how property becomes a social phenomenon.

The scientific process begins with mere mental speculation and, provided there is sufficient truth content in the speculations, ends with tentative knowledge of the world. Given competent reduction to practice and diligence in registration, management, application, tracking and clearing, intellectual property functions like all other forms of property in society. If it is clearly defined in tangible terms, it needs no external regimentation to earn the universal respect, privacy and security required to facilitate stable, peaceful, productive and voluntary social arrangements. Remarkably, intellectual property is turned into knowledge as an outcome of the scientific method.

This monograph is a heuristic exercise aspiring to set forth the content of a course of studies of the prospects indicated in the title. It is complete to the point of repetition in some areas of inquiry and, no doubt, deficient in others. There are abundant hyperlinks in the text and over 400 explanatory notes and bibliographic references listed at the end of the document to aid the reader's comprehension and to support the author's arguments. Since this monograph has so many citations of relevant published information and works of others, the reader is advised to study the work in its digital form, which allows access to most of the works cited with no more than a keystroke.

Readers of this monograph will find the subjects *intellectual property, inductive thinking* and *scientific method* combined into one thesis topic. I intend to show them how these separate ideas actually integrate into one observable natural phenomenon, namely knowledge.

Introduction

The subjects *intellectual property, inductive thinking* and *scientific method* have been found to combine into one thesis topic. These separate ideas actually integrate into one observable natural phenomenon, namely knowledge.

The elements of observable volitional human behavior that occur in the practice of science in general and social science in particular comprise discrete events that can be perceived by seekers of the truth. By examining certain of these elements separately for clarity, they can then be integrated into one concept via the practice of Bacon's method of searching for a greater understanding of the world in terms of its causes and effects, a procedure now known as the scientific method.

Regardless of the connections indicated, there is some controversy surrounding the meaning of each of these topics. There is even controversy in the steps and procedures necessary in the conduct of science itself. These are reasons enough to examine each of these topics separately, all the more especially considering the importance of each on its own merits. But to find connections between them is especially compelling since such an integration would have even greater value, as will be shown.

It is a rare opportunity to find connections between fundamental concepts spanning the social, biological and physical domains of experience without succumbing to reductionism.[122] But alas, this short-cut to the truth is a false hope. Epistemology demands searchers for social knowledge look for regularities in relevant, actual, observable social experience. Principles based on simpler physical experience alone cannot capture the full reality of social phenomena.

Intellectual property happens to be the primary factor in this inquiry because its genesis is at the root of the scientific process—observation. Intellectual property consists of the ideas about future possibilities based on the generalizations of past experience of individuals possessing a functional brain equipped with the power of induction. The scientific process proceeds very nicely on the initiative of these individual intellectual beings wired to become property owners by virtue of their ability to perform the inductive thinking that generates the speculations that motivate scientific effort.

In this introduction, I have made some audacious claims with radical implications, not least the realization that society functions and grows as a natural volitional phenomenon notwithstanding the contrivance and promotion of adversary institutions by

248 | American Polymath

deviant members of the same human population. In other words, society proceeds quite nicely all by itself in a population of ordinary human beings behaving naturally according to their individual inclinations and state of learning within their own sovereign provinces.

Society always exists to some extent and the speed with which it grows in terms of scope and level of activity depends on the tolerance of the population to aggressive onslaughts of parasitic and antisocial political scheming. But society has the advantage in this competition because it is the only place where goods and services are created and offered, promises are kept and eagerly exchanged, and expropriation is righteously resisted.[123] Politics impairs social evolution because all its promises are fraudulent and the frauds cannot be concealed indefinitely. As they eventually come to light, they are resisted to minimize loss and overcome to realize profit. Political expedients eventually fall of their own inadequacy and irrelevance.

By following my upcoming arguments supporting these claims, the reader will be engaged in a heuristic exercise, which is designed to facilitate the tracking of an argument, not so much to persuade as to provoke inquiry and stimulate learning. In doing so, I hope he will be encouraged to question, learn, discover, understand, and solve problems on his own by experimenting with and evaluating the effects of my provisional answers or solutions by using his own thinking and experience. This effort will acquaint him first-hand with the practice of the scientific method. There is also a chance that a theory of society will emerge to the satisfaction of a skeptical and scientifically discerning reader. In that case, progress will have been made toward accrediting an authentic theory of human society.

This monograph is regarded as an exploratory exercise of a prospective scientific treatment of social phenomena based on the universal integrity of individual ownership of property as a trial hypothesis. The subject is developed from an exploration of the consequences of individual man's faculty of induction that produces intellectual property to its role as the prerequisite subject-matter of science, which is the theme of social life in general. This exploratory effort is pursuant to a belief that social progress depends on the perfection and mastery of a dependable social technology, which is paced by advances in an authentic natural science of society.

First published: August 17, 2018
The unabridged monograph is available at, https://www.alvinlowi.net /constructing-a-science-of-society/.

This short article deals with applying the scientific method to society, which Al defined as, "the natural outcome of a population of autonomous, naturally-behaving human beings each endowed with a unique creative spirit of their own." Al insisted, "there is a physical aspect to society that is epistemologically compatible with the laws of physics, specifically the First and Second Laws of Thermodynamics." He then used those laws to show the value of "proprietary communities," aka "entrepreneurial communities," in reducing entropy and increasing order in the world.

Here is Al's version of the laws:

The First Law of Thermodynamics: You can't get something for nothing!

The Second Law of Thermodynamics: You can't even do that well!

The Thermodynamics of Natural Society

The thermodynamic concepts of work and entropy can be validly extended across epistemological boundaries to explain the progressive consequences of voluntaryism and the detrimental effects of coercive regimentation in society.[124] Society based on individual autonomy, strictly voluntary laissez faire human action, and spontaneous order is referred to here as "natural society." [125] Society under the thumb of government regimentation is crippled relative of true society and engenders the inception of a refuge for free enterprise known as an underground, or "black," market.

Many philosophers and classical economists object to any application of any aspect of physical science, or its method of acquiring knowledge of the world, to social studies. They insist that the application of the method of the natural sciences requires the performance of controlled experiments on its subjects, which would be anathema to human actors. Of course, they are right to object to the regimentation of any human by other humans for any purpose. But they are mistaken about controlled experiments in science. If that were so, legacy sciences like astronomy and paleontology would not qualify.

Overlooked is the fact that there is a physical aspect to society that is epistemologically compatible with the laws of physics, specifically the First and Second Laws of Thermodynamics.

An example of the ultimate manifestation of natural society is a business known as a proprietary community. This is a profit-seeking business that derives its return on capital from the income earned from providing community services and accoutrements on parcels of land. Heath and MacCallum have brought this phenomenon to light, which they refer to as an entrepreneurial community (*Entrecom* for short) in their considerable research to support their depth of understanding of its full significance for human freedom and autonomy.[126] In an unpublished paper originally drafted back in 2010 and resurrected in 2019, Lowi and MacCallum depart from the standard coverage of the Entrecom phenomenon and open a way to connect that innovation with the present argument.[127]

That argument suggests that a comprehensive application of the thermodynamic theory of entropy reversal can be applied to an assessment of the global physical consequences of society. Entropy is understood in common terms to be a measure of order in the world.[128] Its numerical value is inversely related to order. So, an increase in entropy actually indicates an increase in disorder, which is related to an increase in scarcity and dysfunction, life-limiting conditions.

Since all genuine economic activity is a natural, volitional human phenomenon, it is observable and understandable via scientific methods. It follows that such activity is technological in nature, i.e., it is a dependable derivative of authentic natural science, teaching humans how to get along and advance their lives in the real world without conflict. Notwithstanding the fact that technology can be used for destructive purposes, it is via technology that the voluntary way of life increases order and human prosperity in the world. A proper natural science of society supports a dependable social technology that develops as scientifically informed entrepreneurs undertake new ventures and enter the market.[129] *Laissez faire capitalistics* is such a technology. [130] And the work associated with the application of that wholly voluntary technology is consistent with the thermodynamic concept of work, which is understood to be the agency for the creation of new order in the universe. Such an increase in order is understood to cause a reduction of the world's entropy. Should any coercion arise in the process, conflict will occur as the victims naturally react negatively to irrationality resulting in the creation of the disorder that increases the world's entropy.

Questions arise as to the cause of coercion and the effect it has on society. This much is clear. Coercion is naturally drawn into play by those ambitious to control the behavior of others, especially when they are overcome with envy of successful entrepreneurial activity. This predatory animal behavior gives rise to opportunities for theft, usurpation, misdirection and expropriation, acts that are absolutely contrary to human cooperation. Unfortunately, initiative coercion incites reactive coercion: old-fashioned justice recognized from antiquity in the

Bible as "an eye for an eye", the outcome of which is that all are blinded.

This natural reaction to circumstances comes from persons acting expeditiously without sufficient knowledge aforethought. As coercion occurs, it is met by another natural phenomenon, namely, the natural reaction to coercion, which is also a resort to force resisting the initiated compulsion to comply with arbitrary directives. It is this impulsive behavior that can never be sufficiently informed to take an alternative voluntary course of action because the initiator of such action has no use for such knowledge, making reciprocity impossible. The initiator is bound and determined to substitute his judgment for that of others who are the exclusive experts regarding their own personal affairs. This is the intractable dilemma that forever dooms initiative government. And in that regard, coercion is like water running downhill, smoke rising and such other natural phenomena that increase the entropy of the universe.

The great physicist Erwin Schrödinger explained in his little book What is Life? how life works to increase lifespan, species longevity and the population of the species. He suggests this is the result of the unique ability of living organisms to regenerate their vital organs and reproduce organisms in kind. These feats of creative work result in entropy reduction associated with the improvement in health and the indefinite extension of the life within a given species. But Schrödinger overlooks the unique entropy-reducing work that occurs with the human species in creating the society described above. That is, the voluntary work that is capable of the extraordinary entropy reduction associated with the ultimate extension of individual human life, indefinitely.

Entrepreneurial community, the "Entrecom," was discovered, elaborated and enhanced by Heath and MacCallum.[131,132] The Entrecom is an example of a social phenomenon that produces a wholesale reduction of the world's entropy. This feat is a result of the establishment of an environment free of taxation and regimentation for multitudes of entrepreneurs engaging in new ventures. Their growth and multiplication are inherent when unmolested by arbitrary government interference, as is the case with all free, proprietary enterprises that are competently managed, putting forth their products in the free market with new innovations and continuous adaptation to growing and changing markets. All that activity qualifies as entropy-reducing work in the manner of classical thermodynamics.

The thermodynamic concepts of work and entropy add insight into the nature of real social progress. In that regard, thermodynamics can be validly extended across epistemological boundaries to explain the progressive consequences of voluntaryism and the detrimental effects of coercive regimentation in society.

First published: February 3, 2021
This article is available at, https://www.alvinlowi.net/the-thermodynamics-of-natural-society/.

Al wrote several articles on global warming. He didn't deny climate change; what he did was try to show: (1) it isn't caused by humans; (2) government intervention does more harm than good.

(1) The activities of industrious humans take place on only a small fraction of the Earth's surface. Local in execution and in sensible effect, only in the fullness of time do the effects of human activity reach the vast fluid volumes of the oceans and atmosphere, and then only after much time has passed and the effects diluted to infinitesimal proportions.

(2) Legislation aimed at curtailing carbon emissions by humans has been rationalized as a proper government application of the so-called precautionary principle. However, inasmuch as it would definitely impoverish humanity without a chance of accomplishing an iota of global environment protection, it seems an odd way for government to do its duty.[133]

In "The Green Energy Boondoggle," Al insisted, "The so-called 'climate crisis' is an empty headline. It is not that climate changes do not occur or that they cannot cause social crises when they do. . . . The reality is that human social practices are too benign physically to cause irreversible global climate changes." To justify these unpopular positions, he went into the science behind his conclusions in minute detail. Readers may not agree with Al's conclusion, but they have to account for the facts he presented in their alternative.

The Green Energy Boondoggle
Abridged

Introduction

Of all the cockamamie political schemes being foisted upon the people of this country by political activists at the present time, the one that vexes me the most is the so-called Green New Deal. This program, funded by the federal government ostensibly to save the environment but actually to exploit pure political opportunity, is the most expensive venture ever undertaken by the federal government other than war. However, like war, it is of no real value to the community or the nation.[134] Also like war, it aims to eliminate by force if necessary the facilities and uses of fossil fuels deemed culpable for a trumped-up emergency known as the climate change crisis.[135] If it seems incongruous that something as frivolous as a "boondoggle" could come out of something as ominous as a "crisis," and then carry such import as to precipitate another crisis, then you are beginning to see the paradigm of politics—one crisis brings another, separated by boondoggles in-between.

Propaganda or Fact?

The so-called "climate crisis" is an empty headline. It is not that climate changes do not occur or that they cannot cause social crises when they do. Hurricanes, tornadoes, heat waves and deep freezes occur in this country with regularity, always taking a toll in human suffering but seldom producing a global social crisis or an irreversible planet-wise climate change. The reality is that human social practices are too benign physically to cause irreversible global climate changes. Whatever doubt ever existed in this matter should have been driven away by Copernicus back in 1543 when he convinced Pope Clement VII to give up the ego- and geocentric notions that justify human supremacy in the cosmic order.

Nevertheless, even a groundless rumor can produce a public panic if it is handled by sufficiently skillful propagandists. I wager such a stunt has precipitated the green energy boondoggle. That misconstrued program aims to dismember one of the great marvels of the modern world in a technically doomed attempt to eliminate carbon emissions from the system without which the society we know literally disappears. It's a fact that energy consumption per capita correlates with the standard of living and the mean life span. That public energy service has been a strictly economic matter explains how such conditions have been achieved. The green energy boondoggle has fomented and imposed technical handicaps on the existing energy system to "level" the energy playing field to the advantage of renewables. The misrepresentation of the carbon emission consequences is a key feature of this boondoggle.

The Green Energy boondoggle is not economic. It is an experiment in government, conceived and administered by politicians. Its implementation unavoidably impaired, and in some instances deliberately sabotaged, the quality of economic public energy service inflicting serious damage to the economy and living standards, especially at the margins. The social disruptions attributable to the renewable energy boondoggle are especially untimely considering the stresses and dislocations associated with the concurrent Chinese corona virus pandemic. Thus, a made-up climate crisis is turned into a real social crisis.

. . .

Cause and Effect

The anthropogenic CO_2 "theory" of Earth-warming asserts human burning of fossil fuels is the cause of environmental changes detrimental to the public welfare. The human connection is essential for green-lighting government intervention. Ambitious politicians have to be seen as protectors in order to proceed without objection from others. Then, government expansion can proceed without rancor to concentrate on controlling such comprehensive human affairs as the energy business.

By now, the climate change panic that prompted the green boondoggle has gone well past the "Chicken Little" stage. Adherents claim the science is settled but there hasn't been an open forum on the scientific evidence of this supposed phenomenon in more than twenty years. News media and scientific publications have been turning away letters and articles having the slightest air of skepticism on the issue. Authoritarianism has become so strong now that if someone in a white lab coat addressed as "doctor" says a proposition is settled science, laymen under the spell of the newscaster will be treated like stenographers taking dictation—they are expected to write "Anthropogenic Global Warming (AGW) is here" into memory as the gospel, like "the sun always rises in the East." They want you to accept their greenhouse religion as fervently. Any inquiry at all skeptical about the holy AGW proposition is officially dismissed without the courtesy of a reply. Dismissals are "scientifically" justified as defenses against deniers, troublemakers or worthless exhibitionists.

It is well publicized by now that the CO_2 in the atmospheric has been increasing, rapidly in recent times. The AGW proposition asserts that this CO_2 rise is causing the global temperatures to rise (see the following chart). [136]

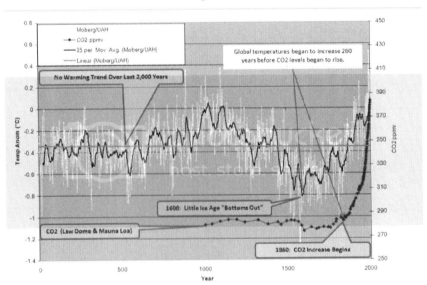

The AGW hypothesis asserts that it is the human fraction of the CO_2 emissions that are sufficient to cause global warming. No evidence is presented to support this assertion. But as seen in the data presented above, this assertion makes the AGW hypothesis a classical fallacy of the type post hoc, ergo, propter hoc (after this, therefore, because of this).

However, note the global temperatures began to increase 260 years before CO_2 levels began to rise. Thus, the official temperature history contradicts the anthropogenic hypothesis, which asserts that the Earth's surface temperature increases **as a result of** the increase in CO_2 in the atmosphere. The truth is the reverse. Whatever the causal connection if any, the CO_2 rose well before the temperature. No distinction was made as to the source of the CO_2 in this chart. But 1860 was well before the beginning of the petroleum age. So, little of this CO_2 could have had an anthropogenic source.

Actually, the CO_2 increased after a perceptible temperature increase, and there is no mystery as to where the CO_2 came from. The oceans contain the greater part of the CO2 on the Earth's surface. This data is also consistent with the physics that calls for a time lag between the temperature rise and the CO2 rise due to the Earth's specific heat and latent heat capacity. The CO_2 was released from the oceans well before human fuel burning could have been a factor.

This data clearly shows the oceans to be the most powerful source of CO_2. The oceans are a vast reservoir of CO_2, normally in equilibrium with the ions in solution and the atmosphere. This CO_2 is from all sources but primarily from submarine volcanoes from below along the many fault-lines demarking the boundaries of the continental plates. The new CO_2 in the atmosphere comes from volcanic activity, soil weathering, vegetation decomposition and fossil fuel utilization, largely in that order. Most of the volcanic emissions stay in the oceans because most of the volcanic fissures are submarine and CO_2 is highly soluble in water. The CO_2 moves from the region where its partial pressure is higher to where it is lower. This means an increase in atmospheric CO_2 due to fuel burning will be temporary because it will be mitigated by diffusion into the oceans.

The question remains as to the source of the heat that produced this temperature rise shown in the chart. Regardless of the sun, the Earth is being heated geothermally in a cycle measured in centuries. The Earth's surface is warmed from underneath to cause the oceans to share more of their carbon with the atmosphere. CO_2 emissions from that source have been strengthening the Earth's atmospheric greenhouse effect since at least 1800 with no significant help from humans. The data show the Earth surface is presently in the heating phase of a geothermal cycle during which the oceans are expanding, the glaciers are receding, and sea-level is rising. There is no reliable data available that shows storms are increasing in frequency and intensity as evidence of climate change.

As shown, until about 1860, the Earth's temperature cycled between heating and cooling while the CO_2 remained steady. The temperature peaked in 1100 AD and bottomed out at about 1600, a 500-year of cooling known as the Little Ice Age, after which it began a warming trend. That trend, which seems to be still in progress, began at least 200 years **before** the onset of the industrial age. This historical fact—along with the fact that the CO_2 took an upward course toward an increase in atmospheric concentration was at least 260 years before human-generated CO_2 would become a noticeable fraction of the atmospheric total—combine to directly refute the AGW hypotheses and discredit the Green New Deal.

. . .

Three pertinent questions remain:

(1) How much of the total CO_2 in the atmosphere is anthropogenic?

(2) What is the CO_2 contribution to the greenhouse effect as a whole? And,

(3) How much of the Earth's temperature rise is due to the greenhouse effect?

Regarding question (1): At present, CO_2 comprises about 0.04% of the atmosphere (400 ppm). But only about 3 to 4% of this amount is of anthropogenic origin. Contrast this puny >0.002% of the atmosphere from human industry with upwards of 4% of the atmosphere that is non-anthropogenic water-vapor. Thus, there are over 2000 times as many heat radiation absorbing water molecules per unit volume of the atmosphere than the human-produced CO_2 molecules.

Regarding question (2): Besides the 2000 times as many water molecules in the atmosphere, consider that the heat absorbing power of each water molecule is far greater than that of the CO_2 molecules. This difference is illustrated in the following graphic.

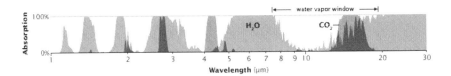

This chart compares the spectral absorbance of the two main atmospheric greenhouse gases in the infrared (heat) spectrum where retention of the Earth's heat content occurs. Note the CO_2 can absorb heat radiation only in very small openings in the "windows" left by the much denser and broader-absorbing water vapor. While the absorption of the heat energy of the Earth occurs only in specific wavelength (color) bands, it is radiated by the Earth's surface continuously across the entire infrared wavelength range because the surface acts as a "blackbody."[137]

The Earth's heat can escape into space by radiating through the small "windows" (white spaces) in the atmosphere provided by the gaps in the absorption spectrum of water (blue bands) cramped slightly by the absorption bands of CO_2 (red bands). Since the absorption shown here is on a "per molecule" basis, the effect of the concentration of the gas in the atmosphere is not seen. That effect would show up as a density of the colors in the bands. For example, where the water absorption overlaps the CO2 absorption, the latter red graphic would disappear under a dense blue graphic representing an eclipse of CO_2 by water vapor. Seen from this perspective, the minuscule effect on heat absorption attributable to this CO_2 is not a plausible candidate for upsetting the thermal equilibrium of the planet.

Regardless of the human contribution, the atmospheric CO_2 does not have a significant effect on the greenhouse strength. In any case, the greenhouse strength is not comparable to the Earth's geothermal heating. The Earth has to radiate more heat to space than it absorbs from the sun in order have a stable surface temperature.

The oceans contain about 50 times more CO_2 than the atmosphere and 19 times more than the land biosphere. To maintain thermal equilibrium, the CO_2 moves daily back and forth between the atmosphere and the oceans by molecular diffusion, driven one way by the sun and in the reverse direction by nocturnal radiation to space. Part of whatever is added to the atmosphere from industrial fuel burning and other such sources is shared with lakes and oceans by such diffusion. Since atmospheric CO_2 is a major plant nutrient, the growth of forests and grasslands mirror the level of atmospheric CO_2 and exert a strong influence on what remains in the atmosphere.

Because the oceans contain so much more CO_2 than the atmosphere, and the partial pressure of CO_2 in the water increases exponentially with the ocean surface temperature, the atmospheric CO_2 is controlled mostly by the ocean temperature. Because over 70% of the Earth's surface is covered by the oceans, an imperceptible ocean temperature increase will drive the CO_2 from the oceans into the atmosphere. This is the phenomenon illustrated in the first graphic. Such emissions occur at a far greater rate than occurs from industrial fuel burning. So, the atmospheric CO_2 is actually driven by the ocean temperature, not the reverse by the sun via greenhouse strengthening from human fuel burning.

CO_2 transport between the oceans and the atmosphere pales in comparison with the diffusion of water-vapor and the subsequent precipitation of water particles. Although water has a lower vapor pressure than CO_2, this is more than offset by its much higher concentration in its source.

Clearly, water vapor is responsible for the Earth's greenhouse effect. Moreover, that gas has a compound effect on the Earth's heat balance. Water vapor is unique in its property to condense into liquid at ordinary temperatures. It is subject to saturation at some particular local temperature limiting the number of vapor molecules that can contribute to a greenhouse effect. Then, those water molecules that condense coalesce into droplets that form clouds, aerosols and precipitation. These particles scatter sunshine back into space before it can be absorbed to form heat, resulting in an Earth cooling effect.

The CO_2 in the atmosphere from human industrial activity has a negligible effect on the Earth's greenhouse effect. Moreover, the greenhouse effect on the Earth's temperature is minor in comparison with the Earth's geothermal effect. Consequently, anthropogenic CO_2 cannot be blamed for altering the Earth's temperature balance. If there is a climate change crisis in process, it is not due to human behavior in any way.

Now, we can take stock of this much-hyped connection between the human exploitation of "fossil" fuels and the supposed invariable and irreversible alteration of the Earth's climate in an adverse direction that justifies government intervention in the economy. Any credibility that ever existed in this theory has vanished under the light of examination using available evidence, the first principles of physics and logic. What's left is empty propaganda, which still serves to alarm people to a bogus climate panic designed to enhance political control of the population. As that control becomes more and more effective, the intrusion involved produces real economic harm and social crisis.

Society, as all those living have come to rely upon, cannot exist without a reliable, ample, available and economic supply of electricity and heat available on site on demand. Such an essential artefact of society has existed until now. It evolved over time to its present state of excellence. But now, governments along with sycophantic and opportunistic industries have embarked on a historic, extravagant, world-wide legislative and executive campaign to dismantle and replace this system with a non-equivalent, non-carbon-emitting, renewable, solar and wind generators produced under government mandate and subsidy rather than in response to market demand. Significant market penetration has already occurred leading to large imbalances in daytime and off-peak generation on the grid, not to mention large increases in government debt.

It was never expected that these intermittent generators could serve independently without sufficient electricity storage capacity to supply the grid properly, around-the-clock and calendar, carbon free. Such storage is not presently available, which means the addition of must-take solar generation must displace an equal amount of conventional generation for over a fourth of the day. But without storage, that displaced generating capacity will be required to quickly resume operation as the sun sets until it rises again as if it was never shut down. This part-time mode of operations required for continuous grid electric service is to be provided by what's left of the fossil-fuel-burning generating capacity still operable and serviceable but with increased cost, service interruptions and carbon emissions. As a result, the reliability and availability that had become the hallmark of the traditional utility system is now in tatters. So much for the Green energy boondoggle.

Political government is now running rampant over the industrial economy on the pretense of preventing humans from impairing the habitability of the Earth. Here, we have opened the curtain to the physical reality of the situation to reveal the fraud behind the government's claim of legitimacy and urgency to intrude into human affairs once more. We now know its pretense is totally without merit and its mission is nakedly illegitimate and opportunistic. And we also know that the boondoggles associated with political moves are precipitating changes injurious to the economy and society to an extent bringing on a crisis from unintended economic consequences.

First published: April 2, 2021
The unabridged article is available at, https://www.alvinlowi.net/the-green-energy-boondoggle/.

Other articles dealing with climate and global warming:
The Consequences of Climate Politics, https://www.alvinlowi.net/the-consequences-of-climate-politics/.

Human Control of the Global Climate, https://www.alvinlowi.net/human-control-of-the-global-climate/.

Warming or Cooling?, https://www.alvinlowi.net/warming-or-cooling/.

AFTERWORD

I hope you enjoyed learning about my dad, an American Polymath, as much as I enjoyed helping this book about him become a reality. I am his firstborn. He already had twenty-four years of interesting life experience by the time I came along. I didn't realize how interesting and remarkable his life experiences were until I was quite grown up. But as it often is for a child, your parents don't seem like real people in the same sense as everybody else. It takes until you grow up and possibly have kids yourself that the nature of your parents' personalities becomes clear.

As a dad, Al taught by example. He brought a sense of calm, rationality, and sanity to what, for a child, could feel like a chaotic world. For this I will always be grateful; I felt safe in this world as long as he was near. He was a poster child for embracing change and looking forward. He was curious and always eager to learn something new. He had a big open mind and a big open heart. He challenged us to question ourselves and the world around us. He told us to, "leave the door open and see who walks in." He was forgiving and fair.

One is sometimes asked what you learned from your parents—a piece of advice you received that you will always carry with you. Al provided many, actually; I will share just three that have impacted my life the most.

First, "You can't control another person's behavior." This is a really hard lesson to learn because instinct, or at least desire, might lead us to believe we can. However, such a belief can result in great frustration and disappointment, and accepting this fact, no matter how difficult, leads to an underlying truth of nature.

Second, "Don't look for reasons where there aren't any." This lesson is connected to the first, as one will always look for the rationale behind events and people's behavior to try to understand why things are happening. But sometimes there are no reasons, and herein appears to be another underlying truth of nature.

And third, his saying to me, "You asked for it, Rose," in response to small complaints—my cats keeping me up all night chasing a rat—or in response to large joys—a professional success. By saying this, he's telling me I'm the master of my own ship, autonomous, self-determining; that my intentions, choices, and actions define me and my world. In this way, I am myself a truth of nature.

His death has had a profound impact on all who knew and loved him. Organizing and supporting the development of this biography has gone a long way to comforting us all. I'm also comforted by the fact that a larger audience, by reading this book, will feel the power and joy of this incredible person and be enriched by his ideas and words.

I thought I would feel old knowing I'm only twenty-four years younger than my dad, who passed at ninety-two. But when I think about him, I actually feel quite young. My loving father—my mentor, my hero, my friend—I still don't know how I will face the future without you, but I aspire to follow your example.

—Rosamina Lowi

ENDNOTES

Acknowledgments

1   Mark Twain, *An Autobiography of Mark Twain*, ed. Charles Neider, Perennial Classics (New York: HarperPerennial, 2021), 473.

PART ONE
Chapter 1

2   Dictionary.com, s.v. "Renaissance man," accessed October 11, 2022, https://www.dictionary.com/browse/renaissance-man.

3   *The New Encyclopaedia Britannica* (US: Encyclopaedia Britannica, 1974), 29:282.

4   "Dictionary.com, s.v. "genius," accessed October 11, 2022, https://www.dictionary.com/browse/genius.

5   Walter Isaacson, "What Makes a Genius? The World's Greatest Minds Have One Thing in Common," *Time*, November 16, 2017, https://time.com/5027069/what-makes-a-genius/.

6   Wikipedia, s.v. "polymath," accessed October 11, 2022, https://en.wikipedia.org/wiki/Polymath.

7   John David McKee, The Modern Polymath, *Ins & Outs* (blog), August 23, 2019, https://insandouts.org/the-modern-polymath/.

8   Marquis Who's Who Moderator, "Alvin Lowi Jr.," Marquis Who's Who Top Engineers, August 4, 2021, https://marquistopengineers.com/2021/08/04/alvin-lowi/.

9   Alvin Lowi Jr., "Scientific Method: In Search of Legitimate Authority in Society," March 8, 1998, https://www.alvinlowi.net/scientific-method/.

10   See Alvin Lowi Jr., "The Green Energy Boondoggle," The Collected Works of Alvin Lowi, Jr. (website), April 2, 2021, https://www.alvinlowi.net/the-green-energy-boondoggle/.

11   Lowi, "The Green Energy Boondoggle."

12   Alvin Lowi Jr., "Government Protection," The Collected Works of Alvin Lowi, Jr. (website), April 18, 2021, https://www.alvinlowi.net/essays/government_protection/.

13   Lowi, "Scientific Method."

Chapter 2

14   Dixon Hayes, "Previous Temple Attack in Gadsden Remembered After Pittsburgh Shooting," 6WBRC Fox News, October 29, 2018, https://www.wbrc.com/2018/10/29/previous-temple-attack-gadsden-remembered-after-pittsburgh-shooting/.

15   Elizabeth Berg, *The Art of Mending*, repr. ed. (New York: Ballantine, 2005), 236.

Chapter 3

16   The word actually means a parcel of land or a small plot of cultivated land.

Chapter 4

17   Marquis Who's Who Moderator, "Alvin Lowi Jr." (see chap. 1, n. 8).

18   Walter Isaacson, *The Innovators: How a Group of Hackers, Geniuses, and Geeks Created the Digital Revolution* (New York: Simon & Schuster, 2014), 215.

19   Mike Hamel, *Spencer MacCallum: A Man Beyond His Time* (Colorado Springs, CO: EMT Communications, 2021), 51.

20   Hamel, 52.

21   "Alvin Lowi," ResearchGate, accessed October 12, 2022, https://www.researchgate.net/profile/Alvin-Lowi.

22   "Patents by Inventor Alvin Lowi, Jr.," JUSTIA Patents, accessed October 12, 2022, https://patents.justia.com/inventor/alvin-lowi-jr.

23   Alvin Lowi Jr. and Chas Holloway, "Thorium," The Collected Works of Alvin Lowi, Jr. (website), December 9, 2019, https://www.alvinlowi.net/thorium/.

24   Lowi and Holloway.

25   *Farlex Dictionary of Idioms*, s.v. "illegitimi non carborundum," accessed October 12, 2022, https://idioms.thefreedictionary.com/illegitimi+non+-carborundum.

Chapter 5

26   Alvin Lowi Jr., "On Andrew Galambos and His Primary Property Ideas," Voluntaryist.com, March 31, 1998, http://voluntaryist.com/property/lowi.html.

27   Lowi, "On Andrew Galambos and His Primary Property Ideas."

28   Alvin Lowi Jr., "A Lasting Encounter: Reflections on My Friendship with Andrew Galambos," The Collected Works of Alvin Lowi, Jr. (website), January 8, 2003, https://www.alvinlowi.net/a-lasting-encounter/.

29   Harry Browne, "Andrew Galambos—the Unknown Libertarian," *Liberty*, November 1997, https://www.galambos-fei.com/_files/ugd/87900f_2f341ff5b7594fa9811eb86711bcf95c.pdf.

30   Fred G. Marks and Allison J. Marks, "Andrew J. Galambos: History of Origins of the V-50 and V-201 Lectures," Voluntaryist, accessed October 12, 2022, http://voluntaryist.com/how-i-became-a-voluntaryist/andrew-j-galambos-history-of-origins-of-the-v-50-and-v-201-lectures/.

31   Marks and Marks, "Andrew J. Galambos.

32   Lowi, "On Andrew Galambos and His Primary Property Ideas."

33   Browne, "Andrew Galambos."

34   Charles R. Estes, "We Never Called Him 'Andy': My Recollections of the Person and Philosophy of the Earlier Joseph A. Galambos Alias Andrew Joseph Galambos the Liberal," *Voluntaryist*, no. 78, February 1996, http://voluntaryist.com/articles/078.html.

35   Jay Stuart Snelson, "Andrew J. Galambos, the Free Enterprise Institute, and Freedom," www.galambos-fei.com, August 9, 2009, https://www.galambos-fei.com/_files/ugd/87900f_2a58b1cbb6ba487db1e7bce8f427facb.pdf.

36   Alvin Lowi, Jr., "Voluntary Government as a Marketable Service: Reminiscences on the History of an Idea," Alvin Lowi, Voluntaryist.com, accessed June 6, 2022, https://voluntaryist.com/how-i-became-a-voluntaryist/voluntary-government-as-a-marketable-service-reminiscences-on-the-history-of-an-idea-by-alvin-lowi/.

Chapter 6

37   Alvin Lowi Jr., "Constructing a Science of Society: A Trial Based on the Universal Integrity of Property Principle," The Collected Works of Alvin Lowi, Jr. (website), August 17, 2018, https://www.alvinlowi.net/constructing-a-science-of-society/.

38   Alvin's comments about Spencer Heath are drawn from the following sources: Lowi, "Constructing a Science of Society"; Spencer Heath MacCallum and Alvin Lowi, "A Summary of the Philosophy of Spencer Heath," Libertarian Papers 10, no. 1 (2018), http://libertarianpapers.org/wp-content/uploads/2018/08/post/2018/08/lp-10-1-6.pdf; Alvin Lowi Jr., "The Legacy of Spencer Heath: A Former Student Remembers the Man and Offers Some Observations on the Scientific Orientation of His Work," The Collected Works of Alvin Lowi, Jr. (website), January 3, 2001, https://www.alvinlowi.net/the-legacy-of-spencer-heath/.

39   Hamel, Spencer MacCallum, 5–6 (see chap. 4, n. 19).

40   Hamel, 43–44.

41   See Alvin Lowi Jr. and Spencer MacCallum, "Community Technology: Liberating Community Development," chapter 6 in Cities and Private Planning: Property Rights, Entrepreneurship and Transaction Costs, ed. David Emanuel Andersson and Stefano Moroni (Northampton, MA: Edward Elgar, 2014); and MacCallum and Lowi, "A Summary of the Philosophy of Spencer Heath" (see n. 38, above).

42   Derk Arend Wilcox, Joshua Shackman, and Penelope Naas eds. The Right Guide: A Guide to Conservative and Right-of-Center Organizations: 1993, (n.p.: Economics America, 1993), 108.

43   Lowi, "Constructing a Science of Society." (See pg 243 of this book.)

44   Joseph Gilly, "The Art of Community," Reason, April 1972, https://reason.com/1972/04/01/the-art-of-community/.

45   Lowi, "The Legacy of Spencer Heath" (see n. 38, above).

46   Lowi, "The Legacy of Spencer Heath."

47   Lowi, "Scientific Method" (see chap. 1, n. 9).

Chapter 7

48   Alvin Lowi Jr., "Constructing a Science of Society (see chap. 6, n. 37).

49   Alvin Lowi Jr., "The Natural Science Project of scienceofsociety.net," The Collected Works of Alvin Lowi, Jr. (website), November 3, 2020, https://www.alvinlowi.net/research/natural_science_project_of_scienceofsociety_dot_net/.

50   Lowi, "Constructing a Science of Society."

51   Lowi, "Constructing a Science of Society."

52   Lowi, "Constructing a Science of Society."

53   Alvin Lowi Jr., "No Conceivable Reform," The Collected Works of Alvin Lowi, Jr. (website), November 1, 1998, https://www.alvinlowi.net/essays/no_conceivable_reform/.

54   Lowi, "Constructing a Science of Society."

55   Dictionary.com, s.v. "laissez faire, accessed October 12, 2022, https://www.dictionary.com/browse/laissez-faire.

56   Alvin Lowi Jr., "Natural Society," The Collected Works of Alvin Lowi, Jr. (website), October 13, 2020, https://www.alvinlowi.net/natural-society/.

57   Lowi, "The Natural Science Project of scienceofsociety.net."
58   Lowi, "The Natural Science Project of scienceofsociety.net."
59   Lowi, "Constructing a Science of Society."
60   Alvin Lowi Jr., "Autonomy," The Collected Works of Alvin Lowi, Jr. (website), October 19, 2018, https://www.alvinlowi.net/autonomy/.
61   Alvin Lowi Jr., "Abstention Is Not Apathy: Must We Depend on Political Protection?" The Collected Works of Alvin Lowi, Jr. (website), February 1, 1999, https://www.alvinlowi.net/essays/abstention_is_not_apathy/.
62   Lowi, "Government Protection" (see chap. 1, n. 12).

Chapter 8
63   Lowi, "Constructing a Science of Society" (see chap. 6, n. 37).
64   Lowi, "Constructing a Science of Society."
65   Ernest Hemingway, *Death in the Afternoon* (1932; New York: Scribner, 2002), 218, eBook.
66   Baltasar Gracian, *A Pocket Mirror for Heroes*, ed. and trans. Christopher Maurer (New York: Doubleday, 2011), 61.
67   Wikipedia, s.v., "Danny Kaye," accessed September 13, 2022, https://en.wikipedia.org/wiki/Danny_Kaye#Business_ventures.
68   Danny Kaye, quoted in *Quote Unquote: A Handbook of Famous Quotations*, comp. M. P. Singh (New Delhi: Lotus, 2006), 191.

PART TWO
Politics, Political Science, and Political Technology
69   Alvin Lowi Jr., "Scientific Method."
70   The Random House Dictionary of the English Language, Unabridged Edition, 1966.
71   Theodore J. Lowi, *American Government: Incomplete Conquest*, (Hinsdale, IL: Dryden Press, 1976), 77.
72   Lowi, *American Government*.
73   Nora Sayre, "Fifty Years and Counting: The Power of the Blacklist," *Los Angeles Times*, April 13, 1997, M1.
74   Matt Ridley, *The Origins of Virtue: Human Instincts and the Evolution of Cooperation*, (New York, Viking Press, 1995).
75   James Thurber, "The Fairly Intelligent Fly," *Fables for Our Time*, (New York, Harper and Brothers, 1940).
76   Bruce M. Canter, personal communication, March, 15, 1997.
77   Spencer H. MacCallum, *The Art of Community*, Institute for Humane Studies, January 1, 1970, 86ff.
78   Ridley, *The Origins of Virtue*.
79   Lowi, *American Government*.
80   Arthur Koestler et. al., *Beyond Reductionism: New Perspectives in the Life Sciences* (Boston, Beacon Press, 1969).

The Illusion of Majority Righteousness
81   Alvin Lowi, Jr., "Political Democracy Leads to Kleptocracy, but Economic Democracy Comes to the Rescue," November 24, 2013, https://www.alvinlowi.net/political-democracy-leads-to-kleptocracy/.
82   Lowi, "Political Democracy Leads to Kleptocracy."

83 Henry L. Mencken, *Notes On Democracy: A New Edition*, Afterword by Anthony Lewis, Introduction and Annotations by Marion Elizabeth Rodgers, (New York, Dissident Books, 2007).

84 Theodore J. Lowi, *Incomplete Conquest: Governing America*, (New York, Holt, Rinehart and Winston, 1981) 25.

85 The Nazis rose to power in a politically democratic campaign challenging the aristocrats running the existing Weimar Republic for rule over Germany. Hitler beat von Hindenburg in the 1932 election for Chancellor (President) of the Republic. Democracy was a key element in the appeal of Hitler's Nazis who were much more adept at democratic politics than von Hindenburg's old Prussian aristocrats. Hitler appealed to popular economic and cultural values that had been suppressed by the victors in the aftermath of WWI.

86 "spontaneous order," https://en.wikipedia.org/wiki/Spontaneous_order.

87 Ludwig von Mises, *Human Action*, (Yale University Press, 1949). Murray Rothbard, *Man, Economy and State*, (D. Van Nostrand Co., 1962).

88 Lowi, "Political Democracy Leads to Kleptocracy."

Abstention Is Not Apathy

89 George Carlin, *A Modern Man*, (New York: Hachette Books, 2021), 166.

90 Lowi, "No Conceivable Reform." (see chap. 7, no. 53).

Rule of Law

91 Lowi, "Constructing a Science of Society."(see chap. 6, no. 37).

92 F. A. Hayek, *The Road to Serfdom*, (Chicago, University of Chicago Press, 1944; New York: W.W. Norton, 1979; Norman, OK: University of Oklahoma Press, 1995).

93 Percy W. Bridgman, *The Nature of Physical Theory*, Princeton University Press, 1936. (See especially Chapter Two - "Operations").

94 Theodore J. Lowi, *American Government: Incomplete Conquest* (Hinsdale, IL: Dryden Press, 1976).

95 Karl R. Popper, *Objective Knowledge*, (London, Oxford University Press, 1972).

Money: The Root of All Good

96 Alvin Lowi, Jr., "Money: An Indispensable Root of Community," The Collected Works of Alvin Lowi, Jr. (website), November 14, 2020, https://www.alvinlowi.net/money/.

97 "Is Money the Root of All Evil?" JW.org, https://www.jw.org/en/bible-teachings/questions/money-root-of-evil/.

98 Fiat money is currency that a government has declared to be legal tender. It is not backed by any physical commodity. Its redeemability ultimately enforced on others by the government it is not backed by a physical commodity. https://www.investopedia.com/terms/f/fiatmoney.asp.

99 Graham Munro, "Autonomics, a New and Improved Digital Money," munro@moneylabs.io.

100 E. C. Riegel, *Flight from Inflation: The Monetary Alternative*, Spencer Heath MacCallum and George Morton, eds. (Los Angeles, CA, Spencer H. MacCallum, The Heather Foundation, 2003).

101 Charles R. Estes, *Voluntary Exchange: The Keystone of Civilization* (San Diego, CA: Mary L. Estes, 1997).

102 John Imig, email to Graham Munro and Alvin Lowi Jr., December 13, 2020.

Economics in Three (+) Pages

103 Lowi, "Constructing a Science of Society." (see chap. 6, n. 37).

104 Henry Hazlitt, *Economics in One Lesson: The Shortest & Surest Way to Understand Basic Economics*, (Harper & Brothers ed., July, 1946); 205 pages. https://fee.org/resources/economics-in-one-lesson/.

105 Art Carden, "Do We Really Need All These Barbecue Restaurants?" American Institute for Economic Research (AIER) Daily Economy, February 16, 2021, https://www.aier.org/article/do-we-really-need-all-these-barbecue-restaurants/.

106 Julian L. Simon (Princeton, NJ: Princeton University Press, 1981).

107 Frederic A. Hayek, "The Use of Knowledge in Society," *The American Economic Review*, September 1945 issue, https://fee.org/articles/the-use-of-knowledge-in-society.

108 E,C. Riegel, *The New Approach to Freedom*, Valun Institute for Monetary Research, New York, 1949; expanded new edition published by the Heather Foundation, San Pedro, CA,1976.

109 Ludwig von Mises, *Human Action*, Yale University Press, first edition, 1949.

110 Spencer H. MacCallum, "Will the Real Golden Rule Please Stand Up?" unpublished essay, June 8, 2014.

111 Adam Smith, *An Inquiry into the Nature and Causes of the Wealth of Nations*, (London: W. Strahan and T. Cadell, 1776).

112 Jay S. Snelson, *Taming the Violence of Faith: Win-Win Solutions for Our World in Crisis* (North Charleston, SC: CreateSpace, 2011).

113 Oscar Wilde, *The Picture of Dorian Gray*.

114 Adam Smith, *op. cit.*, 1776.

115 Andrew J. Galambos, "Capitalism, the Key to Survival, " Course 100, Free Enterprise Institute, Los Angeles, 1961.

116 Spencer Heath, *Citadel, Market and Altar* (Elkridge, MD, Science of Society Foundation, 1957).

The Evolution of Property

117 Spencer Heath, *Citadel*, Market and Altar (Elkridge, MD: Science of Society Foundation, 1957)..

118 Heath, *Citadel, Market and Altar*, 234.

119 Spencer H. MacCallum, "A Wakeup Call for Christian Libertarians: The Teacher of Galilee: A Seer Who Really Did See," Libertarian Christian Institute, August 30, 2017, https://explorersfoundation.org/archive/maccallum-spencer-golden-rule.pdf.

120 E. Adamson Hoebel, *The Law of Primitive Man*, (New York: Atheneum, 1968), 58.

121 Julian L. Simon, The Ultimate Resource, (Princeton, NJ: Princeton University Press, 1981).

Constructing a Science of Society

122 Reductionism is the practice of inappropriate simplification of scientific

investigations of complex phenomena by resort to established understandings of simpler phenomena such as from physics. This turn is an epistemological mistake often committed by searchers for social regularities bent on trying to find short-cuts via the venerated laws of physics.

123 Harry Scherman, *The Promises Men Live By: A New Approach To Economics*, (New York: Random House, 1938).

The Thermodynamics of Natural Society

124 Alvin Lowi, Jr., "The Thermodynamics of Human Progress," The Collected Works of Alvin Lowi, Jr. (website), January 31, 2021, https://www.alvinlowi.net/essays/thermodynamics_of_human_progress_the/.

125 Lowi, "Natural Society." (see chap. 7, n. 56).

126 Spencer H. MacCallum, "The Enterprise of Community: Market Competition, Land, and Environment," *The Journal of Libertarian Studies* 17, no. 4 (Fall 2003).

127 Alvin Lowi Jr. and Spencer MacCallum, "Entrepreneurial Community Development: The Need for Management Integrity," unpublished, 2010, revised in 2019.

128 Alvin Lowi Jr., "Entropy Forever: The Origin of the Concept and Its Significance in Understanding the Utilization of Energy," unpublished, 2012.

129 Alvin Lowi Jr. and Spencer Heath MacCallum, "Community Technology: Liberating Community Development," September 28, 2014, https://www.elgaronline.com/view/edcoll/9781783475056/9781783475056.00013.xml.

130 "Capitalistics" is the proper usage for reference to the technology of voluntary cooperation in the marketplace for personal gain. "Capitalism" is the more common usage referring to an ideology that may or may not be consistent with the technology. The latter term is more often used as a pejorative.

131 Spencer Heath, Citadel, *Market and Altar* (Elkridge, MD: Science of Society Foundation, 1957).

132 Spencer H. MacCallum, *The Art of Community,* Institute for Humane Studies, January 1, 1970,

The Green Energy Boondoggle

133 Alvin Lowi Jr., "Warming or Cooling? You Be the Judge," The Collected Works of Alvin Lowi, Jr. (website), March 1, 2007, https://www.alvinlowi.net/essays/warming_or_cooling/.

134 Dictionary.com, "boondoggle," https://www.dictionary.com/browse/boondoggle.

135 Rahm Emanuel's law of political opportunism: "Never let a crisis go to waste." Until there is a crisis in human affairs, there is no cause of action by political government. No one says the crisis has to be real.

136 "How much of the atmospheric CO2 is anthropogenic?" Debunk House, http://debunkhouse.wordpress.com/2009/11/20/how-much-of-the-atmospheric-co2-is-anthropogenic/.

137 A blackbody radiates and absorbs radiant energy continuously across all wavelengths according to Planck's Law.

ABOUT THE AUTHOR

 Mike Hamel is a storyteller by trade and the author/editor of more than forty-five books on topics as wide-ranging as business, finance, political theory, healthcare, nonprofits, and religion. These include nineteen books for children and young adults. He has written or edited biographies of William Pollard (former CEO of ServiceMaster), Merrill Oster (founder of Pinnacle Forum America), Craig Glass (founder of Peregrine Ministries), Chris Crane (founder of Edify), Scott Boyer (founder of OWP Pharmaceuticals), and Spencer MacCallum (author of *The Art of Community*).

Learn more about Mike on Amazon,
https://www.amazon.com/Mike-Hamel/e/B001JSB7FE/
and Wikipedia, https://en.wikipedia.org/wiki/Mike_Hamel.
You can contact him at emtcom@comcast.net.